THE

PUBLICATIONS

OF THE

SURTEES SOCIETY

VOL. CLXXII

Made and Printed in Great Britain
by Northumberland Press Limited
Gateshead on Tyne

THE

PUBLICATIONS

OF THE

SURTEES SOCIETY

ESTABLISHED IN THE YEAR
M.DCCC.XXXIV

VOL. CLXXII

FOR THE YEAR M.CM.LVII

At a COUNCIL MEETING of the SURTEES SOCIETY, held in Durham Castle on Tuesday, June 7th, 1960, Professor Edward Hughes in the Chair, it was ORDERED—

"That Professor A. G. Dickens' edition of the Clifford Letters should be printed among the Society's publications."

H. S. Offler,
Secretary.

CLIFFORD LETTERS
OF THE
SIXTEENTH CENTURY

EDITED BY

A. G. DICKENS

PUBLISHED FOR THE SOCIETY BY

ANDREWS & CO., SADLER STREET, DURHAM
and
BERNARD QUARITCH, 11 GRAFTON STREET
NEW BOND STREET, LONDON W.1
1962

QUEEN MARY
COLLEGE
LIBRARY

CONTENTS

PAGE

PREFACE 11

CHIEF ABBREVIATIONS 13

INTRODUCTION
- i. The Documents 15
- ii. The Cliffords 18
- iii. The Correspondents 34

THE CLIFFORD LETTERS
1. The Abbot and Convent of Byland to the first Earl of Cumberland [Undated; c. 1525-1526] 57
2. Lancelot, Prior of Carlisle, to the Same, 24 November [1537] 58
3. The Prior and Convent of Furness to the Same, 10 June [? 1531] 59
4. Thomas, Abbot of Holm Cultram, to the Same, 30 August [? 1534] 61
5. John [Norton], Prior of Mountgrace, to Lord Clifford, 27 August [? 1521] 62
6. John [Wilson], Prior of Mountgrace, to the Same, 13 December [1522] 63
7. The Same to the Same, 4 January [1523] 67
8. The Same to the Same [15 March 1523] 70
9. The Same to Henry, Lord Clifford, later first Earl of Cumberland, 27 November [1523] 72
10. Richard Methley, Monk of Mountgrace, to Lord Clifford, 3 October [? c. 1510-1515] 74

PAGE

11. Henry, Abbot of Roche, to the first Earl of Cumberland [Undated; ? c. 1535] 75

12. Richard, Abbot of Shap, to the Same, 26 April [? 1537] 77

13. William, Abbot of St. Mary's, York, to the Abbot of Shap, 6 July [1534] 78

14. The Same to the first Earl of Cumberland, 4 September [1534] 79

15. The Same to the Same, 28 October [1530-1538] 81

16. William Burbanke to Lord Clifford, 18 July [1518] 82

17. Brian Higdon, Dean of York, to Lord Clifford, 3 October [1520] 84

18. The Same to the first Earl of Cumberland, 11 September [? c. 1530] 85

19. Thomas Magnus, Archdeacon of the East Riding, to the first Earl of Cumberland, 24 March [1542] 87

20. Cardinal Wolsey to Lord Clifford, 17 November [? 1518] 88

21. The Same to the first Earl of Cumberland, 20 March [? 1526] 89

22. Copy of a Letter, probably from Lord Clifford to Archbishop Savage, 11 September [1503-1506] 90

23. Anne Clifton to Sir Henry Clifford, later first Earl of Cumberland, 6 March [1518] 93

24. Lady Anne Conyers to the first Earl of Cumberland, 16 June [1538] 95

25. The Same to the Same [4 April 1539, or 26 March 1540] 96

26. Thomas, second Lord Dacre of Gilsland, to Lord Clifford, 6 January [? 1514] 96

27. William, third Lord Dacre of Gilsland, to Sir William Parr, 30 November [1525] 99

PAGE

28. The Same to the first Earl of Cumberland, 16 March [1535] 100

29. Thomas Jolye, Vicar of Skipton, to the second Earl of Cumberland, 7 January 1549 101

30. Henry Algernon, fifth Earl of Northumberland, to the first Earl of Cumberland, 19 April [1526 or 1527] 104

31. Henry Percy, later sixth Earl of Northumberland, to the Same, 16 October [1526] 105

32. Henry, sixth Earl of Northumberland, to the Same, 28 January [1528] 107

33. The Same to the Same [Undated; c. 23 August 1533] 108

34. The Same to the Same, 12 July [? 1532] 110

35. Lady Katherine Scrope to the first Earl of Cumberland, 14 October [1536] 111

36. Lady Katherine Cholmeley, *alias* Scrope, to the third Earl of Cumberland, 20 June [1583-1585] 113

37. Henry, seventh Lord Scrope of Bolton, to the first Earl of Cumberland, 10 August [c. 1530] 114

38. The Same to the Same [Undated; ? c. 1530-1533] 116

39. John, eighth Lord Scrope of Bolton, to the [? first] Earl of Cumberland, 23 February [? 1534-1542] 117

40. The Same to the first Earl of Cumberland, 11 April [1540 or 1541] 118

41. The Same to the Same, 6 June [1540 or 1541] 121

42. John Scrope, later eighth Lord Scrope of Bolton, to the first Earl of Cumberland, 30 October [? 1533] 121

43. Edward, third Earl of Derby, to the Same, 29 August [1536] 123

44. Eleanor, Countess of Cumberland, to the second Earl of Cumberland, 14 February [1543-1547] 125

PAGE

APPENDIX

A Summary of the Lives of the Veteriponts, Cliffords, etc., by Anne Clifford, Countess of Pembroke 127

INDEX OF PERSONS AND PLACES 151

PREFACE

I wish to express my gratitude to Mr. T. C. Skeat of the British Museum, who lightened the first stages of my work by lending me his handlist, with its useful suggestions toward the dating of the letters. I am also much indebted to Dr. R. T. Spence for the loan of his thesis, from which I have gleaned valuable information regarding the lands and family papers of the Cliffords. Dr. A. I. Doyle first encouraged me to edit these letters and then sent me several most erudite and useful notes on the Carthusians, who figure so prominently in this collection.

A. G. Dickens.
The University, Hull.

CHIEF ABBREVIATIONS

Clay	J. W. Clay, *The Extinct and Dormant Peerages of the Northern Counties of England.*
Craven	T. D. Whitaker, *The History and Antiquities of the Deanery of Craven,* ed. A. W. Morant.
Dodds	M. H. and R. Dodds, *The Pilgrimage of Grace and the Exeter Conspiracy.*
Dugdale	W. Dugdale, *Monasticon Anglicanum,* ed. J. Caley, H. Ellis and B. Bandinel, edn. 1817-30.
G.E.C.	G. E. C[okayne], *Complete Peerage,* revised edn. by V. Gibbs.
Glover's Visitation	*The Visitation of Yorkshire . . . by Robert Glover* etc., ed. J. Foster.
L. & P.	*Letters and Papers, Foreign and Domestic, of the Reign of Henry VIII,* ed. J. S. Brewer, J. Gairdner and R. H. Brodie.
Lollards and Protestants	A. G. Dickens, *Lollards and Protestants in the Diocese of York 1509-1558.*
New Eng. Dict.	*The Oxford English Dictionary*, ed. J. A. H. Murray.
Nicholson and Burn	J. Nicholson and R. Burn, *History and Antiquities of the Counties of Westmorland and Cumberland.*
Reid	R. R. Reid, *The King's Council in the North.*
Test. Ebor.	*Testamenta Eboracensia* (vol. iv, *Surtees Soc.*, liii; vol. v, *ibid.*, lxxix; vol. vi, *ibid.*, cvi).
Valor Eccles.	*Valor Ecclesiasticus,* ed. J. Caley and J. Hunter.
V.C.H.	*Victoria County History.*
Y.A.J.	*Yorkshire Archæological Journal.*
Y.A.S. Rec. Ser.	*Yorkshire Archæological Society, Record Series.*

INTRODUCTION

I. THE DOCUMENTS

Of the forty-four letters printed below, forty-one are addressed to successive heads of the house of Clifford, while the remaining three also relate closely to the affairs of that once great North Country family. Though the immediate provenance of the collection remains obscure, one may scarcely doubt that at some juncture it must have been withdrawn from the family archives. Assuming our attributions to be correct, nine of these items were directed to Henry Clifford, tenth Baron Clifford (*c.*1454-1523); twenty-nine to his son Henry, first Earl of Cumberland (1493-1542); two to Henry, the second Earl (1517-1570) and only one to that most famous of all the Cliffords, the flamboyant Elizabethan adventurer George, the third Earl (1558-1605). With only three or four exceptions, our letters derive from the reign of Henry VIII. Of the twenty-eight correspondents represented, the vast majority, it is true, merely give the day and month of writing, omitting the year. Such provincial letters often prove difficult to date, since they refer with much less frequency than the statepapers to national events and well-documented persons. Yet after due search and reflection, internal clues enable us in many cases to deduce the precise year and in most others to establish a strong probability or a close approximation. On this basis it would seem that one item dates from the years 1503-1507; six from 1510-1519 and no less than thirty from 1520-1539, those two decades so fateful in the history of northern England. A further six were written during the forties, while only one is Elizabethan. In the broadest terms, we thus present a collection illustrating noble and clerical life in the north on the eve of the Reformation and during its early stages. Though the letters prove distinctly informative upon the state of the English Church and its relationship with lay interests, they provide little direct evidence concerning the social and spiritual changes commonly grouped under that capacious blanket-word 'Reformation'. Yet by the same token, the letters afford a broad prospect of the real Tudor world; they are not a selection of 'illustrative' documents abstracted by some modern doctrinaire historian prone to impose his own patterns of thought upon a former age.

How did this particular group come to be separated from the main Clifford collections? The evidence at present available to the editor unfortunately does not warrant even a conjectural answer. From the death of the fifth Earl in 1643, the family papers underwent a steady process of separation, and today they lie in many repositories. The Westmorland estate documents remain at Appleby Castle; those for Craven were donated in 1956 to the Yorkshire Archaeological Society; those for Bolton Priory and Londesborough have joined the Duke of Devonshire's collections at Chatsworth. Many private, official and household papers are also at Appleby and Chatsworth, or else with Earl Spencer's manuscripts at Althorp.[1] However voluminous in the aggregate these records remain, it seems all too likely that a great number of others have disappeared in relatively recent times. Several papers noticed or printed in 1805 by T. D. Whitaker in his *History of Craven*, and then at Skipton or Appleby, cannot now be traced. On the other hand, our present group of letters was unknown to Whitaker and so had presumably become detached at some earlier date. In June 1955 it suddenly emerged from a private collection at one of Messrs. Hodgson's booksales, but the record of this sale has not enabled the present editor to trace the previous owner. Acquired by the British Museum, it has been bound in a single volume and numbered Additional MS 48965. It should here, however, be stressed that, with only one exception, the manuscripts are the actual and original letters; the exception (no. 22) is quite naturally a copy, being the only 'outgoing' letter, and incidentally the only one of the collection written by a head of the house of Clifford.

In March 1957, Mr. T. C. Skeat published in the *British Museum Quarterly*[2] a five-page article drawing attention to various points of interest. This valuable but brief contribution apart, we now encounter materials quite new to Tudor historians;[3] today it affords an uncommon pleasure to bring to the press a collection of this scope and interest lying quite outside that most comprehensive of all calendars for an English reign, the *Letters and Papers of Henry VIII*. Our

[1] For further detail on the main Clifford collections, see R. T. Spence, *The Cliffords, Earls of Cumberland, 1576-1646* (London University, Ph.D., 1959), pp. xii-xiv.

[2] Vol. xxi, no. 1, pp. 4-8.

[3] Apart from nos. 43 (printed in 1890 from a copy and with an incorrect attribution) and 35, printed by Mr. Skeat in his article cited *supra*.

documents may owe their preservation, and indeed their abstraction from an earlier group, to some unknown reader's interest in their authors, nearly all of whom are persons of distinction or special interest. The collection has also been bound by the British Museum upon a basis of authorship and not upon chronological principles. The present editor sees no adequate reason to depart from the arrangement by correspondents, except in the cases of nos. 40 and 41, which have been interchanged, since they come not merely from one author, but refer to the same matter and should be read in the sequence of their dates. Otherwise, the items have been left with the same order and numeration as those of the manuscript volume. We thus begin with fifteen letters from the heads of northern religious houses and then six more (nos. 16-21) from eminent secular clergy, including Wolsey. With these it might have been defensible to place no. 29, the writer of which has proved on further investigation to have been a vicar of Skipton. This one apart, nos. 22 to 43 all come from members of the northern noble and gentle houses, arranged by families: Clifford, Conyers, Dacre, Percy, Scrope and Stanley. Of all these varied correspondents, the great majority signed letters written by their secretaries. Certain of our few lay autograph letters, notably those by Henry Percy, later sixth Earl of Northumberland, (no. 31) and Anne Clifton (no. 23) stand in sharp contrast with the neat work of the clerical writers, so chaotic is their handwriting, so luxuriant and erratic, even by Tudor standards, their orthography.

Letter 44, written to the second Earl by his wife Eleanor, niece of Henry VIII, is a 'stray' item formerly at Appleby Castle and not a part of the collection in Additional MS 48965. Like the latter, however, it has not yet found its way into print. Its writer, character, period and intrinsic interest make it a most proper and desirable addition to our series.

As an appendix we print Lady Anne Clifford's *Summary* of the lives of the Shepherd Lord and of the first two Earls. Based largely upon records no longer extant, this narrative forms our most important background-document. It has often been cited incorrectly or incompletely, and only its subsequent portions were printed by the Roxburghe Club.[4]

In reprinting all these texts, the original spelling has been preserved, while punctuation and capitalisation have been modernised. Some of the more debatable expansions, together with the few 'restorations'

[4] Cf. *infra*, p. 150.

necessitated by damage to the manuscripts, are enclosed in square brackets. Though our texts have been repeatedly checked against the originals, a collection so miscellaneous precludes absolute infallibility and consistency of detail. Yet only readers unfamiliar with the strange vagaries of Tudor correspondents will assume that the quite 'improbable' spellings necessarily arise from errors of transcription.

II. THE CLIFFORDS

It was Robert, first Lord Clifford and the true founder of his house, who acquired the manor of Skipton-in-Craven: most readily we associate the family with the austere Pennine landscape and with Skipton Castle, the frowning symbol of Clifford territorial power. Even so, until the sixteenth century the great bulk of their lands lay in Westmorland and came from Robert's maternal ancestors the Viponts. The centre of gravity began to shift southward into Yorkshire when the ninth Lord—the 'Butcher' of the Wars of the Roses—married Margaret Bromflete, since this heiress brought to her descendants not only a questionable claim to the title of Lord Vescy but considerable lands in the East Riding. With her son, the so-called 'Shepherd Lord', the Tudor phase of Clifford family history commences.[5] Since Wordsworth wrote *The Song of the Feast of Brougham Castle*, the more romantic episodes of this baron's life have been widely known. His father having been slain by a stray arrow on the eve of Towton, the victorious Yorkists granted his lands to Richard Duke of Gloucester, Sir William Stanley and others.[6] Henry, tenth Lord Clifford, then aged about seven, lay in real danger and was brought up first as a shepherd on his mother's estate of Londesborough; later, with the help of Sir Lancelot Threlkeld of Yanwath, he was smuggled into an even greater obscurity in Cumberland. The story, told below in detail by Lady Anne Clifford,[7] deserves credit, since in its broader outlines it goes back to Edward Hall.[8] At the same time, it may well be that Clifford's concealment did not

[5] The chief works of reference are: G.E.C., especially iii. 293-5 and 566 *seqq.*; *D.N.B.*; J. W. Clay in *Y.A.J.*, xviii. 355 *seqq.*; *Craven*, especially pp. 311 *seqq.*; *Lives of Lady Anne Clifford*, ed. J. P. Gilson (*Roxburghe Club*, 1916); G. C. Williamson, *George, Third Earl of Cumberland, 1558-1605*, and *Lady Anne Clifford*; R. T. Spence, *op. cit.*

[6] References in *Y.A.J.*, xviii. 370-71.

[7] *Infra*, pp. 133-4.

[8] Hall, *Chronicle*, edn. 1809, p. 255.

last so long as Lady Anne suggests: at all events on 16 March 1472 he received a pardon from Edward IV, wherein he was recognised as heir, not indeed to the Clifford estates, but to those of his maternal grandfather Lord Vescy.[9] In November 1485 his attainder was clearly reversed and his estates restored by Act of Parliament.[10] His mother Margaret, having married Sir Lancelot Threlkeld, survived until 1493, and her attractive brass with its inscription[11] setting forth her titles still graces the church of Londesborough in the heart of the Vescy estates.

Lord Clifford's public career is well documented. He was summoned to Parliament from September 1495 to November 1514; visited London in October 1494, when Prince Henry was made a Knight of the Bath, and again in June 1509 for the coronation. He helped Surrey in 1497 to relieve Norham[12] and fought in the central vanguard at Flodden,[13] whence he bore off three of King James's cannon to decorate Skipton Castle. He frequently appears in official records as a commissioner of array for Cumberland, Westmorland and the three Ridings. Of Westmorland, like his forbears and his successors, he occupied the hereditary sheriffwick. Toward the French expedition of 1522 he lent no less than 1000 marks, one of the highest sums on the list.[14] His financial situation, so much more auspicious than that of the Percies, must have owed much to his avoidance of court life and expensive public duties. Lady Anne Clifford relates that her great-great-grandfather grew to be very rich 'in money, chattels and goods and great stocks of ground', being 'a plain man', who lived for the most part a country life and came seldom to court or London, except when called to Parliament.[15] Most of his charters are dated at Barden Tower,[16] that now picturesque ruin overlooking one of the lovelier stretches of the Wharfe. Wordsworth does not stray far from historical fact in recording Clifford's devotion to astronomy, astrology and alchemy,

> 'Most happy in the shy recess
> of Barden's lowly quietness',[17]

[9] *Cal. Pat., 1467-77*, p. 327.
[10] I Hen. VII cap. 5.
[11] Printed in *Craven*, p. 323.
[12] *Anglica Historia of Polydore Vergil* (*Camden Ser.*, lxxiv), ed. D. Hay, p. 99.
[13] Hall, *op. cit.*, p. 557; *Craven*, p. 326. He was then over 60 years of age.
[14] *L. & P.*, iii(2). 2483(2).
[15] *Infra*, p. 135.
[16] *Craven*, p. 324.
[17] *The White Doe of Rylstone*, lines 293-4.

and in recounting his collaboration with the Augustinian canons of nearby Bolton. In the catalogue of Ralph Thoresby's library is a manuscript *Treatise of Natural Philosophy in Old French* given by Henry Lord Clifford to Bolton Priory and reverting to the family after the dissolution.[18] Again, Whitaker saw among the family manuscripts an English treatise in verse and prose concerning alchemy, followed by some Latin books on astronomy. This he dated about the time of Henry VII, and from the English portion he quoted passages to support his contention that it possessed Craven dialect-characteristics and derived from the canons of Bolton.[19] The likelihood is strengthened by the fact that the writer addresses his audience as 'Fathers' or 'Worshipful Fathers'. Though the present location of this group of manuscripts does not appear to be known, another from the same background survives among the Skipton papers now in the library of the Yorkshire Archaeological Society. This is a substantial fragment of the *Compound of Alchemy* written by George Ripley, another Augustinian, though of Bridlington, and dedicated to Edward IV. The work was not printed until 1591, but this manuscript probably belongs to the early years of the century.[20] Yet another 'scientific' manuscript thought to have belonged to Lord Clifford is a commentary on the works of the Arab physician Ishak ibn Sulaiman al Israeli; it dates from *c.* 1300 and is at Appleby, having originally been found at Skipton.[21] Nevertheless we cannot profess certainty that every one of these manuscripts belonged to the Shepherd Lord, since his grandson the second Earl of Cumberland was also, as will appear, addicted to alchemy and kindred studies.

Lord Clifford first married Anne St. John of Bletsoe, Bedfordshire, a cousin of Henry VII and famed alike for tapestry-making and piety. From this union sprang his heir Henry (b. 1493) and his second son Thomas, who was ultimately knighted, became Governor of Berwick and held various other northern appointments.[22] Having also begotten

[18] Catalogue of MSS in Thoresby, *Ducatus Leodiensis*, edn. 1816, p. 90, no. 186. Its history is here said to be recorded by 'some verses made by the second Earl before his marriage with the Lady Eleanor, daughter of Charles Brandon, Duke of Suffolk, by Mary Queen of France'.

[19] *Craven*, pp. 324-5, 473-7.

[20] Y.A.S., Skipton Papers, bundle 109. On Ripley see *D.N.B.* and corrections in A. B. Emden, *Biographical Register of the University of Oxford*, iii. 157.

[21] Described in *Trans. Cumb. and Westm. Antiq. Soc.*, xviii. 94. This was in 1917; the present editor has not inspected this volume.

[22] *Y.A.J.*, xviii. 372-4 gives many particulars of him.

two or three illegitimate children, Lord Clifford ultimately embarked upon a second marriage with Florence, widow of Thomas Talbot of Bashall in Craven, and by birth a Pudsey of Bolton-by-Bolland and Barforth.[23] This marriage produced two or three sons who died young, and a daughter who married Sir Hugh Lowther of Westmorland.[24] In September 1522 Lord Clifford was so 'feebled with sickness' that his eldest son—usually known in these years as Sir Harry—had to lead the Clifford contingent in the Scottish campaign.[25] He died on 23 April 1523, and was buried either at Shap Abbey or at Bolton Priory, to both of which houses he had been a notable benefactor.[26]

During his later years the old Lord's relationship with his heir had been strained to breaking-point by the extravagant and disorderly conduct of the younger man, who, nurtured at court alongside the future Henry VIII, had clearly diverged from his father and from his northern responsibilities. He also quarrelled with his step-mother, Lady Florence.[27] On the subject of his misdeeds, his father wrote a long and angry letter to an unnamed member of the King's Council.[28] Here Lord Clifford recalls that he has shown his correspondent and others of the Council 'the ungodly and ungudely disposition of my son Henrie Clifforde, in such wise as yt was abominable to heare it'. Sir Harry had flouted his commands, had threatened his servants with destruction after his death, had struck and perilously injured his old servant Henry Popely, had spoiled his houses and stolen his goods. All this arose through malice and inordinate pride, which had made Sir Harry leave the court for the country, clothe himself and his horse in cloth of gold and goldsmith's work, 'more lyk a duke than a pore baron's sonne as hee ys'. By the King's command, the writer had given his son £40, urging him to forsake the dangerous counsels of certain evilly-disposed young gentlemen. Lord Clifford had already complained in violent terms to the King and his councillors, denouncing his son for seeking maintenance of certain great lords 'in his countree'. The offender had nevertheless continued to

[23] On Lady Florence, cf. *infra*, pp. 131-2.

[24] Cf. *infra*, p. 132.

[25] *L. & P.*, iii(2). 2524.

[26] Cf. *infra*, p. 136. The formal burial seems to have taken place nearly a year after his death. Cf. *L. & P.*, iv. 227, which must certainly be dated 5 April 1524, not 1523, as Williamson supposed. Cf. *infra*, p. 136, n. 35.

[27] *Infra*, p. 135.

[28] *Craven*, p. 327 prints the letter, attributing it to Lady Anne Clifford's memoranda at Appleby.

sow dissension between the gentlemen, 'and troblith divers housys of religion, to bring from them ther tythes, shamfully betyng ther tenaunts and servants, in such wyse as some whol townes are fayne to kepe the churches both nighte and daye, and dare not com att ther own housys'. It seems obvious even from this one-sided account that the father's stinginess had helped to provoke the son's revolt, but there can be no doubt that the future first Earl of Cumberland was living a wild life when approaching the age of thirty.[29] Though the letter is undated, we know roughly when these exchanges were taking place and something of their sequel. Thomas Leeke, presumably of the well-known Derbyshire family, wrote from the Fleet prison on 25 October 1517 to his brother Sir John, showing that Sir Henry Clifford and Sir George Darcy had recently been incarcerated there with him. Sir Henry recommended himself to Sir John Leeke, having been 'a prisoner here this fortnight and he is waxen a sad gentleman'. Last Friday Clifford and Darcy had been before Cardinal Wolsey at Hanworth; he had liberated them on account of the plague, but had taken no pity on the writer, Thomas Leeke.[30] While the latter had no certain connection with Clifford's offences, Sir George Darcy, son of the hero of the Pilgrimage of Grace, may well have been one of the 'evilly-disposed gentlemen' against whom the elder Clifford had complained. Even at this stage of his career the young man appears to have enjoyed some success in building up an independent income. In October 1518 Lord Dacre jealously pointed out to Wolsey that Sir Henry Clifford then drew from the King's lands in Yorkshire 100 marks, and had £60 in Craven 'by means of Sir John Carr'.[31] The latter had been High Sheriff of Yorkshire three years earlier and probably influenced the grant of offices and leases to Clifford.

However disorderly his conduct in Yorkshire, Sir Henry must indeed have used his opportunities at court not only to gain stewardships but to develop that close friendship with the young King which dated from their childhood. When in 1523 he succeeded to the baronage,[32] he lacked the dangerous attribute of over-popularity in the north, and yet he controlled an interest large enough to help counterbalance those of the Percies, the Nevilles and the Dacres.

[29] The birth of his illegitimate son Thomas Clifford must have been somewhat earlier, since Thomas was deputy-captain at Carlisle in 1537 (*L. & P.*, xii(1). 419).

[30] *Hist. MSS Comm., 10th Report*, App. iv. p. 447.

[31] *L. & P.*, ii(2). 4541.

[32] He had livery of his lands 18 July 1523 (*ibid.*, iii. 3190).

Whether or not these precise calculations influenced the King in elevating him on 18 June 1525 to the earldom of Cumberland, Henry must confidently have expected faithful service. In the event, his hopes proved well-founded, since by this stroke he enlisted a new northern champion to the cause of law and order. He could not, it is true, eradicate that harsh and grasping disposition which Cumberland continued to manifest to his dying day. The new Earl began by refusing to pay for the customary illuminated patent, and Garter King of Arms had to present merely the signed bill when he took his seat.[33] The expense-roll for this journey to London[34] shows that he was profuse in personal adornment, very economical in his alms-giving, and not very liberal in choosing a present to take home to his countess. This lady and her offspring play a by no means inconsiderable part in our letters. Clifford's first marriage with a daughter of the fourth Earl of Shrewsbury had been terminated by her very early death, and about 1516 he had been matched with Margaret Percy, eldest daughter of the 'Magnificent' fifth Earl of Northumberland. The strength of the link which the pious and kindly Margaret formed between the two houses will in due course become manifest.

Matters stood very differently in relation to the Dacres, whose feud with the Cliffords[35] seldom flagged throughout the Earl's lifetime. After the death of Thomas Lord Dacre in 1525, Cumberland took over not only the wardenship of the West March and the captaincy of Carlisle, but also every stewardship and lease which could be wrested from the Dacres and their adherents.[36] In 1528, after the young sixth Earl of Northumberland had failed to compose their quarrel,[37] the King's Council in the North imprisoned four of William Lord Dacre's servants for assaults upon Cumberland's tenants, and urged Wolsey to adjust matters between the two magnates.[38] In December 1531 some junior members of the Dacre family began an affray against the Earl and his relatives in Carlisle.[39] Early in 1534 Lord Dacre himself was accused of march treasons, Cumberland taking a

[33] *Trans. Cumb. and Westm. Antiq. Soc.*, xviii. 198.

[34] *Craven*, pp. 329-334.

[35] It is traditionally supposed to have developed through the elopement of Thomas Lord Dacre with the heiress Elizabeth Greystoke, at that time in the care of the Cliffords at Brougham (R. S. Ferguson, *Hist. Cumberland*, pp. 160-6).

[36] *L. & P.*, iv(i). 1763. Cf. the disputes over the delivery of Carlisle in 1525 (*ibid.*, 1762 and *infra*, p. 48).

[37] *L. & P.*, iv(2). 3971. Cf. *infra*, no. 32.

[38] *Ibid.*, 4855; cf. *ibid.*, 4790.

[39] *Ibid.*, v. 573.

leading part in the enquiries and in attaching his goods.[40] Though Dacre was acquitted by the Lords,[41] there followed prolonged wrangles concerning the restoration of his property, and in the December Thomas Cromwell intervened to impose an award upon the two families.[42] In the same year the Earl resumed the wardenship of the West March, and thenceforth for many years the Clifford interest stood predominant in Cumberland and Westmorland.

Though not conspicuously generous or gracious toward the Church, Cumberland remained entirely conservative in his religious outlook. In October 1530 he founded a guild in honour of Our Lady and St. John in the parish church of Skipton, requesting the fallen Wolsey's confirmation of its ordinances.[43] Alongside those eminent conservatives the Duke of Norfolk and the Earl of Shrewsbury, he proved a staunch Henrician, signing the Divorce petition to the Pope[44] and serving as a commissioner at the trials of More, Fisher, and the prior of the London Charterhouse.[45] His close relations with the dynasty also appear in the royal marriage which he arranged in that same year for his heir, the bride being Lady Eleanor Brandon, daughter of Charles, Duke of Suffolk and the King's sister Mary, ex-Queen of France. In order to prepare for the advent of this highly-born daughter-in-law, Cumberland built the great gallery of Skipton Castle.[46] The story of his defiance of the Pilgrimage of Grace has already been told in great detail by M. H. and R. Dodds. Froude also related with gusto, but with numerous errors, the story of Christopher Aske, who, aided by the vicar of Skipton and a boy, rescued the Lady Eleanor and certain of the Earl's own daughters from Bolton Priory, thence leading them by stealth through the midst of the rebels into the safety of Skipton Castle.[47] The Askes and the Cliffords were in fact related[48] and Christopher had been employed by the Earl as one of his agents.

[40] *Ibid.*, vii. 679, 680; Dodds, i. 35; Reid, p. 118.

[41] The indictments and verdicts are fully summarised in *L. & P.*, vii. 962.

[42] *Ibid.*, 1549; cf. *ibid.*, 1365, 1588, 1589. The award is corrected in Cromwell's hand, but it was probably drawn up in the first place by the King's Council in the North; cf. no. 28 *infra*.

[43] *Ibid.*, iv(3). 6677.

[44] *Ibid.*, 6513.

[45] *L. & P.*, viii. 886, 974(i).

[46] *Infra*, p. 141. For her jointure see 27 Hen. VIII, private acts, cap. 8; *L. & P.*, x. 243(8).

[47] Froude, *Hist. Eng.*, ii. 553-4.

[48] *Craven*, p. 335 gives an illustrative genealogy.

To the solid basis of agrarian discontent which underlay the Pilgrimage, the Earl contributed by his unpopular enclosures. In the previous summer of 1535 these had occasioned violent riots among his tenants at Giggleswick and elsewhere.[49] Lord Darcy may have been a prejudiced witness, but he did not greatly err when he said 'that my lord of Comberland is in great parell of his lyf, for if the comens myght gette hym, they would kylle hym, for he is the worst beloved that ever I hard of, and specially with his own tenants, and yf ther be no remedye founde, I thinke he can not escappe'.[50] Even the Duke of Norfolk thought him 'greedy to get money of his tenants'.[51] In mitigation, it may be said that he was not the only enclosing landlord in the area,[52] that his harshness may have been aggravated by mere agents on remote estates, and that, in sending the names of the leading rioters of 1535 to Cromwell, he pointed out that they were poor men and urged that they should merely be released and a few bound to appear before the Council.[53]

In January 1537, Cumberland's loyal service earned for him a place on the Council in the North,[54] but otherwise no shower of offices fell upon him; perhaps the government realised that such a development would increase unrest, since the Cliffords were now as closely beset by feuds and tensions as any of the great northern families.[55] The year which followed the Pilgrimage is notable rather for the advent of 'new' men like Bishop Holgate and the first Lord Wharton, men whose powers depended directly upon the King and not upon territorial influence. On the other hand, the Earl's last years saw great extensions to the Clifford estates in Yorkshire. The first of these arose from his marriage with Margaret Percy, whose parents had promised her as dowry the Percy Fee in Craven, and whose brother the sixth Earl of Northumberland ultimately settled the Fee

[49] *L. & P.*, viii. 991. On the character and extent of this rising, see also *ibid.*, 863, 892-3, 970, 984, 992-4, 1008, 1030, 1046; *ibid.*, ix. 150, 196, 371.

[50] Somerset Herald's account of his interviews with Darcy, printed in Dodds, i. 305. For Star Chamber cases arising from the Earl's alleged oppressions, see *Yorks. Star Chamber Proceedings*, iii (*Y.A.S. Rec. Ser.*, li), pp. 200-202, and the cases noted *infra*, pp. 59-60.

[51] *L. & P.*, xii(1). 919.

[52] *L. & P.*, viii, 991, 1046; Reid, p. 124; *Yorks. Star Chamber Proceedings*, ii (*Y.A.S. Rec. Ser.*, xlv), pp. 178 *seqq.*

[53] *L. & P.*, ix. 150.

[54] Reid, pp. 150, 491.

[55] Cf. Dodds, ii. 103, 252-3.

upon the future second Earl of Cumberland.[56] Duly confirmed by Act of Parliament, this settlement brought to the Cliffords all the western half of Craven.[57] In 1540 Cumberland purchased Carlton, Lothersdale, Bradley and Utley, four manors in the Aire Valley south of Skipton.[58] He leased in the same year the site and other extensive former properties of Bolton Priory.[59] In April 1542 he purchased these, together with other monastic lands, for £2,490 and a small annual rent of £19.[60] Of the thirteen manors involved in this grant, eight lay close to Skipton. The day before it was completed, he made his will, mentioning that he had already paid in part for the Bolton lands, and specifically bequeathing them to his heir. Again, the religious phraseology of this document remains purely conservative and it provides for requiem masses on a large scale.[61] When the Earl made it he was 'somethinge crased in bodie but holl of mynde'. He died three weeks later (22 April 1542), aged about fifty. The vivid portrait-brass on his tomb at Skipton includes the figure of the Countess Margaret, who had predeceased him in November 1540. This brass is described and illustrated by Whitaker,[62] who also obtained permission in 1803 to examine the family vault below. He found the Earl's coffin much corroded and exhibiting the skeleton of a short and very stout man, with long flaxen hair gathered in a knot behind the skull. The coffin of the Countess indicated that she had been slender and diminutive, while the skeleton of her daughter-in-law Eleanor, as befitted a child of Charles Brandon and a niece of Henry VIII, proved to be that of 'a tall and large-limbed female'.[63]

Henry, second Earl of Cumberland, may be mentioned more briefly, since his affairs occupy but a small section of our documents. The expenses arising from his ambitious marriage are said to have weighed heavily upon his finances and obliged him to sell the ancient Clifford manor of Tenbury in Worcestershire.[64] Lady Anne Clifford, who wrongly regarded the Lady Eleanor as a 'great fortune' (i.e.

[56] *Craven*, p. 12; *infra*, p. 138.
[57] *Craven*, pp. 12, 335.
[58] R. T. Spence, *op. cit.*, p. 9 cites Skipton MS A/29/1.
[59] *L. & P.*, xvi. 1500 (p. 721).
[60] *Craven*, p. 335; *L. & P.*, xvii. 283.
[61] *Y.A.J.*, xviii. 375-9; *Test. Ebor.*, vi. 127-30.
[62] *Craven*, pp. 432-3.
[63] *Ibid.*, p. 429.
[64] *Infra*, p. 148. The Cliffords were tenants there by 1200. Cf. *V.C.H., Worcestershire*, iv. 365.

heiress), may have been over-censorious in calling her grandfather 'a great waster of his estate' in his earlier years. At all events, he left a very substantial inheritance of more than 46 manors, and throughout his career tended to sell isolated estates, both in Yorkshire and elsewhere, in order to purchase lands near his great nucleus in Craven.[65] After the death of the Lady Eleanor in 1547 he suffered a severe illness, being actually laid out for dead, when his watchful servants noticed signs of life and revived him.[66] From this point he retired to his estates and visited the court only thrice: for Queen Mary's coronation, for his daughter's marriage to Lord Derby, and again soon after Elizabeth's accession.[67] About 1552-3 he healed the feud with the Dacres by marrying Anne, a daughter of William, third Lord Dacre, who throughout her life 'was never at London, nor near it, but applyed herself in domestick and home affairs, while she was maid, wife and widow'.[68] Both the Earl and his second father-in-law were thought to hold reactionary religious opinions and both were accused in 1561-2 of encouraging Romanism in the north.[69] There seems little doubt that, before the rising of 1569, Cumberland led the Northern Earls and the Dacres to expect his active support. In the event, he either lost nerve or changed his views, and though some of his tenants rallied to his brother-in-law Leonard Dacre, the Earl himself assisted Lord Scrope to fortify Carlisle against the rebels.[70] This confusion was caused or aggravated by poor health; he is described at this moment as 'a crazed man' and he died very shortly afterwards, in January 1570.[71] Gentler and more intellectual than his father, the second Earl shared some of his grandfather's interests. According to the Lady Anne, he was 'a great distiller of waters and maker of chemical extracts, very studious in all manner of learning'. And she adds that he possessed 'an excellent library of books, both

[65] A feodary survey of 1573 shows the total value of the Clifford estates as £1,821, above reprises. Of this sum the Yorkshire estates (the vast bulk of them in Craven) produced £1,092, those of Westmorland £580, those of Cumberland £24 and the manor of Hart in Durham £120. Cf. R. T. Spence, *op. cit.*, pp. 11-14, 381-3.

[66] This and other lively details are given by Lady Anne *infra*, p. 149.

[67] *Infra*, p. 149.

[68] *Infra*, p. 146.

[69] Froude, *op. cit.*, vii. 19, 21.

[70] References in *D.N.B.*

[71] Cf. C. Sharpe, *Memorials of the Rebellion of 1569*, p. 70. Dr. G. C. Williamson, *George, Third Earl of Cumberland*, p. 3, supports Lady Anne's date, 8 January 1570, as the date of his death.

handwritten books and printed, to which he was addicted exceedingly, especially towards his latter end'.[72]

The life of George, third Earl of Cumberland, cannot be claimed as part of the background to this collection; he figures merely as the recipient of one letter, which tells us nothing about him. In any case, since the publication of Dr. G. C. Williamson's attractive biography, he has become one of the more familiar figures of Elizabethan England.

We may now briefly review our new evidence concerning these successive heads of the house of Clifford. With regard to the 'Shepherd Lord', the most interesting letters are those which delineate his relations with the Carthusian priory of Mountgrace.[73] Though this house lay far from his main estates, its piety had earned it a wide regional prestige throughout all Yorkshire, and the fact that it attracted Clifford's patronage should occasion no surprise. Letter 5 shows him financing the building operations of the house at some date not long before the death (? 1521) of Prior John Norton. Here Norton accounts to him for the expenditure of his money and refers to these activities as 'Goddes work and yours'. They continued with increasing momentum under Norton's successor John Wilson, who wrote nos. 6, 7 and 8 in 1522-3. In the first of his letters Wilson also consults Clifford on the purchase of lands, part of these being intended to endow an 'anchorage' or hermitage for the welfare of the elderly baron's soul. Wilson also urges Clifford to complete his various gifts to Mountgrace before death should overtake him. It also transpires that Clifford has an affection for John Neville (Lord Latimer's son, and later husband of Katherine Parr) and wants Neville to act in trust for him, apparently in connection with his monastic benefactions.

To this new information we may here add a fragment recently culled from the manuscript records of the Carthusian order. The General Chapter which assembled at the Grande Chartreuse on 25 April 1524 included in its list of obits: *Honorabilis vir dominus Henricus de Clifforde, baro et magnus fautor ordinis qui construxit in domo Montis Gracie de novo quinque cellas monachorum*. In the following year the correct date of Clifford's death, 23 April 1523, was also entered in these records of the General Chapter,[74] so that his

[72] *Infra*, p. 149.

[73] The personalities at Mountgrace are described *infra*, pp. 34 *seqq*.

[74] Bibl. Nat., Paris, lat. 10890. I owe this information to Dr. A. I. Doyle. On the monachate purchased for Clifford, cf. *infra*, no. 7. On Clifford's benefactions to Bolton and Shap, cf. *infra*, p. 129.

name could be inscribed in the right space of the calendars and obituaries of the various houses, to which this information was circulated.

In letter 7 Clifford is seen trying to secure for his chaplain a place among the Carthusians. With but a few weeks to live, he is also paying the order for a monachate for himself and giving charitable support to the indigent mother of a deceased monk named John Mylde. In letter 8 Prior Wilson asks Clifford's counsel concerning lands insecurely conveyed to Mountgrace, and now reclaimed by the kinsmen of the late Prior Norton. He provides further information on his building-work and reveals that Clifford has just bestowed upon the house the large sum of 1,000 marks.

Nearly five years before these Mountgrace letters came one (no. 16) from Wolsey's secretary William Burbanke,[75] showing how the Shepherd Lord in his retreat at Barden kept in touch with the world-news of 1518. He learned here of the detailed plans then being made to receive Cardinal Campeggio, the precise significance of Wolsey's new title *legatus a latere*, the impact of the war between the Grand Turk and the Sophi of Persia upon the brave new Christendom and the perpetual peace in the West to which Wolsey's circle aspired. Letter 20, though in Burbanke's hand, comes from the Cardinal himself, and it asks Clifford to supply oaks from his park at Whinfell for a chapel which Burbanke proposes to found at Greystoke, his birthplace. In no. 17 we find that Clifford has presented an unlearned clerk to his benefice at Londesborough and thus has attracted a rebuff from Brian Higdon, Dean of York, who politely refuses to admit such an ignoramus.

The only letter of our series written by a head of the house of Clifford is no. 22, which affords an interesting glimpse of the Shepherd Lord's manorial administration. Though an unsigned and unaddressed copy, it seems to us written between 1503 and 1506 to Archbishop Savage. In the manor of Carlton, one of those which Clifford leased in 1503 from the crown, he found a tenant named John Dale, who defied his wishes and stirred up rancour amongst his fellow-tenants. Though expelled from his holding, Dale continued to give trouble and was finally imprisoned by Clifford at Skipton Castle; not, according to Clifford, in the dungeon but in a 'fair chamber', allowing free access by his friends. On his release, Dale

[75] On Burbanke cf. *infra*, p. 39.

protested to the Archbishop, who had in former years been intimately concerned with the management of the crown lands. Our letter 22 is Clifford's reply to the Archbishop; though it refuses to restore Dale's lease, it is couched in mild terms, and if its facts are approximately true, it could not be adduced as convincing evidence of oppressive landlordism on Clifford's part.

In letter 26, it emerges that the long Clifford-Dacre quarrel was being vigorously waged in 1514,[76] since here Thomas, second Lord Dacre, complains that Clifford has sent his servants Thomas Wharton (father of the well-known first Lord Wharton) and Henry Salkeld to Appleby, in order to induce the local gentry to restrict their Border-services to Dacre as warden. Dacre tells Clifford that he has not as yet complained to the King, but he threatens to do so forthwith, unless Clifford goes immediately to clear up the confusion and to explain the full extent of the service which the gentry are bound by immemorial custom to provide.

Turning to the larger body of letters directed to the first Earl of Cumberland, we again find a number concerned with the monasteries, but they naturally reveal a harder and more calculating relationship. The one apparent exception is a message (no. 9) from Prior Wilson, asking, some six months after the old Lord's death, whether Mountgrace might buy certain lands to the value of £25, or 40 marks, albeit the price was high. If his Lordship pleased, they would need to pay 100 marks deposit at once and the rest on the completion of the sale next term. Here we obviously encounter no new benefaction by the heir, but simply a decent fulfilment of his father's wishes to found an anchorage or hermitage, and to give land to Mountgrace. This phase past, the monastic letters belong to a world of business. In June 1531 Cumberland pressed Furness for a lease of the lordship of Winterburn near Skipton. The house—apparently without an abbot at this time—begged (no. 3) a respite until 29 September in order to seek advice; if anyone obtained the lease, it should be the Earl. As related in more detail below,[77] the latter had already accepted from a rascally monk forged leases of Furness property. He again extracted from the house the stewardship of its lands in Winterburn. In August 1536 Edward Stanley, third Earl of Derby, wrote (no. 43) that Cumberland was punishing the tenants of Winterburn as their steward; let him desist till the matter be tried, since Derby held the

[76] Cf. *supra*, p. 23, and *infra*, p. 48.
[77] *Infra*, pp. 59-60.

stewardship of all the Furness lands by a grant under the common seal of the house.

When in 1534 Lord Dacre became involved in charges of march-treason, Cumberland did all in his power to assume the Dacre monastic offices and profits. In July he induced his friend the abbot of Shap to urge St. Mary's, York, to grant him the tithe of Bolton in Westmorland, hitherto demised to Sir Christopher Dacre (no. 13). The following September the Earl displayed to St. Mary's a royal grant of the stewardship of its lands in Cumberland, the office having formerly been held by Lord Dacre (no. 14). In August 1534, the abbot of Holm Cultram forwarded (no. 4) to Cumberland the draft of an indenture granting him the stewardship of the abbey, once also among Lord Dacre's offices. With Shap the Cliffords continued to the end their traditionally intimate relationship. As late as 1537 the abbot of this house received instructions from the earl to demand arrears of rent from the Earl's tenants at Sowerby and Brough; in return, the abbot asked him to intervene on behalf of a certain Ralph Frear, who was likely to be ejected from a Byland tenement by the machinations of certain Westmorland gentlemen (no. 12). On occasion a monastery might venture to dun Cumberland himself for arrears of payment. This happened in November 1537, when the prior of Carlisle pointed out (no. 2) that the half year's rent of the tithe of Kirkland payable on 3 May was still outstanding. Only on 22 March had the Earl made the previous payment (ten guineas) due on 30 November 1536. The arrears mentioned in both these letters presumably reflect the chaos consequent upon the Pilgrimage of Grace rather than the normal practices of Cumberland and his tenants. And in relation to the monasteries, the material advantages did not always accrue to the Earl. About 1525-6 he had told Byland he would allow that house to reoccupy its lands at Bleatarn and Warcop a year before his lease of these lands expired; if not, he would compound with the monks for the year. In reply the abbot and convent (no. 1) courteously but firmly informed him that the lease had already become void by the death of the former abbot, who had power to make leases only for the term of his own life. If, however, the Earl would agree to their immediate re-entry, they would in return admit him and his family as brethren and sisters of the chapter, and as partakers of their spiritual suffrages. For want of further evidence, we can only hope that Cumberland duly appreciated the offer of these intangible benefits.

Conflicts over seignorial jurisdiction between lay lords and monasteries might also complicate the issue, as may be seen in letter 15, a complaint by the abbot of St. Mary's regarding the arrest of a felon inside the liberties of the house at Kirkby Lonsdale. The Earl's relationships with the monasteries were not, of course, governed solely by selfish considerations. As 'founder' of Roche, he received from the prior a lengthy report (no. 11) on the misdemeanours of a monk, Thomas Acworth, who had waylaid the Earl at Tuxford in order to engage his sympathies. Again, Dean Higdon corresponded with Cumberland (no. 18) concerning the provision of a more energetic prior for Bolton and the business-management of the small Vescy foundation of North Ferriby in the East Riding. As background to this interesting group of monastic letters on the eve of the dissolution, one interpretative generalisation may perhaps be ventured. However little active enthusiasm for monasticism they displayed, the impulse toward dissolution did not come from such magnates as Cumberland. No evidence suggests that they shared Thomas Cromwell's doctrinaire vision of an 'efficient' secular society, nor was it clear during the decades preceding the dissolution that so sweeping a change would conduce to their material interests. The cash-revenues of the great northern families never corresponded with their obligations or their ambitions, and the innumerable monastic leases and paid offices afforded them a steady and welcome source of income. If by any chance they ever imagined the possibility of buying monastic lands on a large scale, they might well at this stage have preferred the existent situation to the task of raising vast capital sums toward a novel and perhaps insecure investment. The probability remains that they never envisaged the prospect of wholesale dissolution until the actuality was almost upon them. However secular-minded, they continued meanwhile to accept the religious houses as established members of the social family and the business-community: one might criticise the monks, bargain with them, bully them or sponge upon them, yet one did not propose their annihilation.

The first Earl's correspondence with laymen scarcely softens our image of a hard and unsentimental businessman. Further light is thrown by no. 21 upon his behaviour at the death of Thomas Lord Dacre in 1525. Having immediately begun to discharge tenants from leases made to them by the Dacres in the liberties of Cumberland, he received from Wolsey a peremptory order to refrain, pending investigation by the King's Council. After the Clifford-Dacre dispute had been regulated at the end of 1534 by Cromwell and the Council in the North, William Lord Dacre had to send his servants with a special request for the cash which Cumberland had agreed to pay (no. 28). This marked reluctance to part with money also finds illustration in a letter (no. 37) from the seventh Baron Scrope. When it was planned to marry the latter's son to Cumberland's eldest daughter Katherine, the Earl gave two valuable cups in pledge for the payment to Scrope of one hundred pounds. The date for settlement having been fixed by the marriage-contract, Scrope sent two trusty servants to Fountains, in order to receive the money and return the cups, together with an acquittance. Yet no one appeared on the Earl's behalf, and Scrope now 'marvelled', supposing the Earl had 'some gret besynes uppon hande at that day' which had caused him to forget the arrangement. Perhaps Scrope had as yet transacted little business with the Earl, or—much more likely—his astonishment was courteously feigned! On the other hand, the letters (nos. 31, 32, 33, 34) of the unfortunate sixth Earl of Northumberland to his brother-in-law Cumberland reflect some indirect credit upon the latter, since they are couched in unmistakably warm and personal terms of friendship.[78]

Of the two missives certainly addressed to the second Earl, much the more important is letter 29, written from London on 7 January 1549 by Thomas Jolye, vicar of Skipton. Indeed, some readers may find it the most politically interesting item of the whole collection, since it provides a vivid and novel illustration of the manner in which northern feuds were now being pursued in Parliament itself. The vicar relates how, just when he was about to return home from London, Richard Musgrave had brought into the Commons a bill to deprive the Earl of his hereditary sheriffwick of Westmorland. This could only have been, he adds, by the procurement of Thomas, first Lord Wharton, Musgrave's father-in-law. A border chieftain direct from the pages of Sir Walter Scott and already famed as the victor of Solway Moss, Wharton was destined to become ever more notorious for the number and bitterness of his quarrels, not only with the Cliffords, but with the Dacres, the Eures, the Vavasours and other northern families. In our letter Thomas Jolye proceeds to relate how Mr. Fairfax, Sir William Babthorpe and other parliamentary friends of the Cliffords had immediately concerted plans to speak

[78] Cf. *infra*, p. 47.

against Musgrave's bill. They had not only enlisted the support of Protector Somerset himself, but had prepared to drag Wharton and Musgrave into the Star Chamber upon some old grievance, should they persist in their plan to humble the Cliffords. These counter-pressures must have proved successful. Not the least attractive aspect of this letter lies in the concluding passages, where Jolye provides a newsletter of the type expected by provincial magnates from their clients in London. His account of the statutes then before Parliament shows him as curiously insensitive to the momentous importance of this Parliament in the history of the English Reformation.

Another characteristic conflict of family-interests appears in the two letters (nos. 40, 41) from John, eighth Lord Scrope, to the first Earl concerning a dispute with his neighbour and brother-in-law Sir Christopher Metcalfe of Nappa over the master-forestership of the parks and chases of Richmondshire. His case having been carried before the Earl, Sir William Babthorpe and Robert Challoner as commissioners, Scrope attempts to induce them to keep a letter of the Lord Privy Seal from the sight of their own Lord President, Bishop Holgate, and their colleague on the Council in the North, Sir Robert Bowes. These two, insinuates Scrope, are 'speciall freyndes and grete favorers to the saide Christofer Metcalf'. Thanks to the remarkably detailed research of the *Metcalfe Records*, we are able to fit letters 40 and 41 into a most complex story of litigation.

III. THE CORRESPONDENTS

Of the monastic correspondents, by far the most attractive to historians of English religion are the three Carthusians of Mountgrace: Richard Methley, John Norton and John Wilson. The first of these was born in 1451-2, his family name being Firth. Entering the Carthusian order at the age of 25, he soon afterwards wrote his mystical treatise *Schola Amoris Languidi*. In a later book, *Refectorium Salutis*, he describes spiritual experiences which befell him in the year 1487. He received bequests in 1500, 1508 and 1509,[79] but though he may have survived several years after the last date, the unreferenced statement that he died as late as 1528 seems to the present writer almost certainly mistaken. An exponent of the 'sen-

[79] *Test. Ebor.*, iv. 189, 270; v. 5.

sory mysticism', Methley achieved a considerable reputation for holiness throughout Yorkshire. Work is at present in progress upon the three of his treatises which occur in Trinity College, Cambridge, MS 1160.[80] Of these, the *Refectorium Salutis*, a species of spiritual diary, mentions two further works now apparently lost.[81] In addition to this list of works, he compiled useful Latin translations of the *Cloud of Unknowing* and the *Mirror of Simple Souls*.[82] Among the statepapers at the Public Record Office can be found the second half of his *Experimentum Veritatis*, a treatise on the tests which should be applied to alleged supernatural experiences.[83] Along with it is Methley's only work in English, *To Hew Heremyte . . . a Pystyl of Solitary Lyfe now a dayes*.[84] This brief, pleasant little guide for hermits was probably addressed to the one in the Lady Chapel immediately above Mountgrace itself (cf. no. 8). It has already been printed, but with many misreadings, some of them important.[85] In our present collection Methley is represented only by a brief, business-note (no. 10) which suggests that, as a senior monk, possibly as procurator, he was entrusted with important practical affairs of the house. As an undoubted autograph it should prove of value when the various Methley manuscripts come under definitive review; those so far examined by the present writer are not in this hand, and seem the products of a cult among his juniors, the last generation of monks at Mountgrace.

Prior John Norton, to whom we ascribe letter 5, was also an author in the same contemplative tradition as his somewhat older colleague Richard Methley. Some preparatory work has already been done towards an edition of his three surviving Latin treatises, which appear in Lincoln Cathedral Library MS A.6.8: *Musica Monachorum*; *Thesaurus Cordium Vere Amancium*; and *Devota Lamentacio*.[86] In the last of these, Norton describes a vision vouchsafed to him 'on the Friday before the feast of Pentecost in the third year of my entry

[80] Cf. M. R. James, *Catalogue of MSS. of Trinity College, Cambridge*, iii. 176-8. I am indebted to Dom Dominic Gaisford for the loan of his transcript of these treatises.

[81] Cf. D. Knowles, *The Religious Orders in England*, ii. 224.

[82] Pembroke College, Cambridge, MS 221, fos. iv-47v and 49-107. Cf. on the former P. Hodgson in *Early Eng. Text Soc.*, ccxviii, pp. xiv-xv, 173-6, and on the latter C. Kirchberger, *The Mirror of Simple Souls* (*Orchard Books*, 1927), Introduction.

[83] S.P. 1/239, fos. 262-265v.

[84] *Ibid.*, fos. 266-267v.

[85] *Thought and Culture of the Eng. Renaissance*, ed. E. M. Nugent, pp. 388-393.

[86] I am indebted to Dom Philip Jebb for the loan of a transcript.

to this holy religion, that is in the year of our Lord 1485'.[87] He receives mention as executor in the will of a female relative dated 1506[88] and he became prior of Mountgrace in 1509 or early in 1510.[89] Norton probably died between March 1521 and March 1522, since he is recorded as deceased in the records of the Carthusian General Chapter for 1522, which may be taken to cover events within this preceding period.[90] A younger contemporary in the house, who copied Norton's treatises, thrice described him as *sixth* prior of Mountgrace, and though this numbering does not harmonise with the list of priors attempted by modern scholars,[91] the discrepancy may be accounted for by the fact that the first few heads of the house were styled rectors, not priors. Norton's letter in our collection (no. 5) shows him roofing three new cells with lead and buying 230 wainscots at Lord Clifford's expense. From Prior Wilson's letters (nos. 6, 8) we also learn that Norton had sought to purchase land for an 'anchorage' of Lord Clifford's foundation. Again, the prior is shown to have sprung from the well-known Yorkshire family, the Nortons of Bilbrough near Tadcaster. His relative Robert Norton had attempted to alienate to Mountgrace some of the family lands, but now in 1522 the collateral warranty designed to secure the title to the monastery was pronounced inadequate to break the entail, the present heirs denying that they had ever made a release of their rights. This passage in letter 8 incidentally yields a scrap of biographical information concerning two eminent judges of the period, Sir John Port and Sir Anthony Fitzherbert, reputed author of the famous *Book of Husbandry*.[92] These two happened to be on circuit in Yorkshire and, as judges commonly did at the time, gave their opinions on the collateral warrant to Prior Wilson. The fees collected by them for this service were no doubt substantial.

Despite such setbacks, Mountgrace continued to expand in wealth and numbers during the early years of Wilson's priorate. Until the discovery of these letters dated 1522-3 (nos. 6, 7, 8, 9), the full extent

[87] Lincoln Cathedral MS A.6.8., fo. 79v. Cf. R. M. Woolley, *Catalogue of the Manuscripts of Lincoln Cathedral Chapter Library*, pp. 29-30.

[88] *Test. Ebor.*, iv. 92n.

[89] Henry Eccleston still occurs as prior in the Rievaulx Chartulary in 1509, but a prior John figures in the Pardon Roll of 1509-10 (*L. & P.*, i(1). 438(i), m. 15).

[90] Cf. *supra*, p. 28, n. 74.

[91] E.g. in *Y.A.J.*, xviii. 264 and in *V.C.H. Yorks.*, iii. 193; these diverge from one another. In the latter, the insertion of a prior William in 1532-3 is certainly incorrect.

[92] Cf. *infra*, p. 70.

of this prosperity and renown could not be appreciated. The prior had a waiting-list of notable applicants for the next vacant cell and when Lord Clifford sought a place for his chaplain, Wilson reminded him of the severe test of vocation imposed by the strict Carthusian discipline. Mountgrace had at that moment only two vacancies, one of which had been promised to Ralph Malleverer, then commissary to Bishop Fisher and in the event destined to become last prior of the Charterhouse near Hull.[93] The other cell had been promised to Mr. William Stapleton of the Wighill family, but he had just died; after him in order of preference came the sub-prior of Monk Bretton, next the parson of St. Saviour's, York, and lastly a former novice who had suffered a breakdown, but was now cured (as he supposed, by a miracle of Our Lady) and being offered a second opportunity. And only the previous day, Wilson had received yet another application from a Cambridge graduate, who claimed to have been promised a cell during the time of Prior Norton. Altogether, Wilson proves one of our most attractive and informative correspondents, a good deal also being known concerning his later life. Though at first inclined to follow his heroic London colleagues in resistance to the Royal Supremacy, he was finally won over to submission by Archbishop Lee and other Henricians.[94] At the dissolution he was assigned a comfortable pension of £60 a year, together with the house and chapel on the Mount.[95] His vocation nevertheless remained true, and when the Marian government refounded the Charterhouse at Sheen, he reappeared and took his place there, bringing with him two monks and two converses of Mountgrace, the largest single contingent from any one former house to enter Sheen.[96]

By way of counterpoise to the austerity and devotion revealed at Mountgrace, the last abbot of Roche recounts (letter 11) in scathing terms the shortcomings of one of his monks, Dan Thomas Acworth. This man had complained to the first Earl of Cumberland as founder of the house, passing above the head of his abbot. The latter now explains that when Acworth had been given his chance as prior, the affairs of Roche had decayed in his hands, since he would take no

[93] *Infra*, p. 67.

[94] H. Ellis, *Original Letters, third series*, ii. 341-6, 374; E. M. Thompson, *The Carthusian Order in England*, pp. 467-72; cf. *L. & P.*, viii. 963, 1011, 1033, 1038-9, 1069; ix. 49, 99; x. 93, 99, 228; xi. 75; xv. 125. Cf. *infra*, p. 67.

[95] *Y.A.J.*, xviii. 263.

[96] On the refoundation of Sheen, see E. M. Thompson, *op. cit.*, pp. 500-9. The Carthusian obits show that Wilson died at Sheen on 10 September 1557.

pains, and behaved as a temporal man 'usyng ryatt, as schotynges and metynges with any man that wer so disposed'. Lightly regarding any reproof, he had been dismissed from office by a visitor of the Cistercian Order. Elected kitchener, he proved equally disastrous in that office, as the Earl might well ascertain by enquiry among the other brethren. It need scarcely be added that this misfit continued in religion and signed the deed of surrender at Roche in June 1538.[97] Another of our monks who came under controversy was William Thornton, the last abbot of St. Mary's, York. Confirmed in office on 2 March 1530, he continued to hold it until the dissolution of this great and wealthy house in November 1539, when he accepted the magnificent annual pension of 400 marks.[98] In the summer of 1535 he corresponded with Thomas Cromwell in order to prevent Archbishop Lee from visiting his house,[99] but Lee proceeded with his plan and issued injunctions which *inter alia* forbade familiarity between Abbot Thornton and Elizabeth Robinson, a married woman of Overton near York, where the abbot had one of his country houses.[100] On 23 August Thornton sent Cromwell a copy of these 'very strange and strict injunctions' and announced that he would appeal to the King in Chancery. As for the woman with whom it pleased the Archbishop to say he was suspect 'in this mine old age', he had every intention of keeping her away from his house, which she had in fact only visited once or twice during the last half year, in order to dine 'with other notable strangers'. Whether this prohibition had been made out of genuine zeal or merely at the suggestion of his enemies, the abbot undertook to obey; he would even accept the order to wear his habit, 'like one of my cloister brethren', unless Cromwell commanded otherwise. Meanwhile, would Cromwell say nothing to Lee about the proposed appeal; Thornton had no trust in the Archbishop, after this mishandling.[101] Reading these documents, one might well surmise that Thornton was no gross evil-liver, but rather the easy-going, society-loving and luxurious head of a rich house, the type forever

[97] J. H. Aveling, *Hist. of Roche Abbey*, pp. 84-6. His name does not appear in the Roche pension list in *ibid.*, p. 87, and J. Burton, *Monasticon Eboracense*, p. 324, but he could be identical with Thomas Harrison.

[98] Dugdale, iii. 539; *V.C.H., Yorks.*, iii. 111; *L. & P.*, xv. 1032 (p. 552).

[99] See their letters to Cromwell in *L. & P.*, viii. 964-5; ix. 63. A *praemunicio* had been sent the previous September (*Y.A.J.*, xvi. 444-5), and Lee also alludes to Thornton's earlier resistance in the summer of 1534.

[100] The injunctions are in Lee's register, printed in *ibid.*, 446-7, and also in the statepapers (*L. & P.*, ix. 158(2)).

[101] *L. & P.*, ix. 158.

depicted in the *Journal* of his contemporary William More, abbot of Worcester.[102] Abbot Thornton did not rank among the intellectual luminaries of the period; Dr. Rowland Lee writes in 1533 that he accepts the King's claims, 'but hee is not lernyd'.[103] His three letters printed below (nos. 13, 14, 15) suggest that he was cautious and by no means neglectful of the interests of his house during its last years.

Of the secular clerics who wrote to the Cliffords, several deserve special mention. Wolsey apart, perhaps the most interesting is his secretary William Burbanke,[104] whose newsletter (no. 16) to Lord Clifford and whose projected chapel at Greystoke (cf. no. 20) have already attracted our notice. An official letter from Wolsey to the first Earl (no. 21) is also in Burbanke's hand. This priest was certainly of Cumbrian extraction, and it would now appear that Greystoke must have been his native place. As early as 1488 he worked in the service of Bishop Bell of Carlisle, and he was doubtless helped by a relationship with Thomas Burbanke, archdeacon of Carlisle from 1503 to 1520.[105] In 1495-6 he was at Cambridge studying Civil Law, the primrose path to ecclesiastical preferment.[106] In March 1508 the Augustinian priory of Conishead, Lancashire, nominated him as proctor in the diocesan synod of Carlisle.[107] Burbanke then moved swiftly from the periphery to the centre, accompanying Cardinal Bainbridge to Rome as steward and secretary, and there in 1509 initiating a friendship with Erasmus. On 1 June 1512, still abroad, he received the prebend of Fenton in the Church of York.[108] On the mysterious death of Bainbridge, he and his more famous colleague Richard Pace acted as that prelate's executors, and in August 1514 he wrote to Henry VIII the well-known letters charging Silvester de Gigli, Bishop of Worcester, with poisoning Bainbridge.[109] In turn, the bishop defamed his accuser as 'that scoundrel Burbanke'. Leo X, who viewed such brawls with distaste, absolved the bishop and

[102] *Worcestershire Historical Soc.*, xxx; described by D. Knowles, *op. cit.*, iii, ch. ix.

[103] *Lollards and Protestants*, p. 161.

[104] For general accounts of Burbanke see P. S. Allen, *Erasmi Epistolae*, iv. 33; *V.C.H., Cumberland*, ii. 47; James Wilson in *Trans. Cumb. and Westm. Antiq. Soc.*, xv. 35-42. It will be observed that some of the details are rendered uncertain by the presence of at least one namesake.

[105] Le Neve, *Fasti*, ed. Hardy, iii. 249. There was formerly a memorial to Thomas in the church of Greystoke (Wilson, *op. cit.*, p. 39).

[106] Allen, *loc. cit.*, cites Cambridge Grace Book B. i, p. 82.

[107] *Hist. MSS. Comm. Rep.*, xii, app. vii, p. 5. He was then B.C.L. Another of their nominees was Robert Burbanke, notary public.

[108] Le Neve, *op. cit.*, iii. 185; Cooper, *Athenae Cantabrigienses*, i. 41.

[109] Ellis, *Original Letters, first series*, i. 100-106; cf. *L. & P.*, i(2). 3203-4.

soothed Burbanke with an appointment as protonotary apostolic; and on leaving for England the latter was also favoured by letters of recommendation from the cardinals to the King.[110] By 1516 he had become chaplain and secretary to Wolsey, with whom he visited Cambridge in 1520, and received a doctorate in Canon Law.[111] Several further preferments came his way: a prebend of Lincoln in 1518; the archdeaconry of Carlisle in 1520, and another prebend at York in 1524.[112] It was to Burbanke that Erasmus wrote from Louvain his famous letter of 1 September 1520, lauding the qualities of the clergy in Wolsey's household: 'o vere splendidum Cardinalem, qui tales viros habet in consiliis, cuius mensa talibus luminibus cingitur'.[113] Burbanke may have been a fairly frequent correspondent of Erasmus, who mentions a letter from him in 1524[114] and alludes to him two years later in writing to Gardiner.[115] In the service of the Cardinal he undertook important duties; in April 1520, for example, he attested the treaty of commerce between Henry VIII and Charles V.[116] At least six impressions of his seal survive; they all date from February 1525 and are attached to the surrender-deeds of monastic houses, which he helped to dissolve under Wolsey's scheme.[117] During these years he presumably spent little time in his native county, but he is known to have stayed with Bishop Kite at Rose Castle in September 1522, since the bishop wrote to say that he had delayed Burbanke's return, wishing to entertain him in honour of the court.[118] On Wolsey's fall, he continued in confidential service to the King,[119] but did not long survive his master.[120] His letter to Clifford was perhaps motivated by his mundane desire for a grant of timber, but it suggests admirably the discreet and diplomatic character of the writer. Burbanke is concerned to interest the baron and to flatter him by imparting exclusive news, but he is careful in his selection of topics. He has much to say on the formal arrangements

[110] *L. & P.*, i(2). 3177, 3183.
[111] Allen, *loc. cit.*, cites Cambridge Grace Book B. ii, p. 78.
[112] Le Neve, *op. cit.*, ii. 236; iii. 218, 249; *L. & P.*, iii(1). 739, 741. It is possible, however, that some of these references are to the other William Burbanke. Cf. Wilson, *op. cit.*, p. 42.
[113] Allen, *op. cit.*, iv. 333-4.
[114] *Ibid.*, v. 541.
[115] *Ibid.*, vi. 405.
[116] *L. & P.*, iii(1). 739, 741.
[117] *Ibid.*, iv(1). 1137; *V.C.H., Cumberland*, ii. 47; cf. plate facing p. 130.
[118] *L. & P.*, iii(2). 2566.
[119] *Ibid.*, iv(3). 5783 (17 July 1529).
[120] He died aged about 60 in 1531. Cf. Wilson, *op. cit.*, p. 42.

planned for the reception of Campeggio, yet he must have known much more of the inwardness of the Legate's visit than he divulges to his northern correspondent. He displays a firm grasp of world-politics and a convinced desire to establish a lasting peace in Christendom, the alluring vision of Wolsey's circle at this apogee of the Cardinal's career. In reading Wolsey's own letter (no. 20), written on Burbanke's behalf, readers will not fail to enjoy the characteristically portentous conclusion: 'whereby ye shall not oonlie do a thing right acceptable onto Gode, but also unto me right singular pleasor.'

Two of our most important ecclesiastical letters (nos. 17, 18) come from Brian Higdon, another member of Wolsey's group and a notable dean of York.[121] Nothing seems to be known of his career until 1499, when he became a bachelor of Civil Law at Oxford. Practising as a proctor in the Chancellor's court there, he achieved the doctorate in 1506; he functioned as principal of Broadgates Hall in 1505-8, after which he occupied prebends at Lincoln until his death. Meanwhile, however, Higdon came north as archdeacon of York in 1515 and stayed there as dean from June 1516, holding in addition the prebend of Ulleskelfe and several Yorkshire benefices.[122] Appointed chancellor of the Duke of Richmond's council in 1525, he continued in membership after its reconstitution as the King's Council in the North.[123] Having helped to negotiate the Treaty of Berwick in 1526, he presided over the dissolution of the late fifth Earl of Northumberland's household in the following year. While he thus acted as Wolsey's chief agent at York, his brother John Higdon was dean of Cardinal College in Oxford.[124] Dean Higdon belonged indeed to that all-important group of Henrician clerical officials whose training in the Civil Law predisposed them to place the claims of Caesar above those of St. Peter. When the tension between international Church and national State came to a head, such men stood invariably on the side of the latter. In 1533 Higdon played a prominent rôle in persuading the Northern Convocation to answer the problems of the Divorce in a sense favourable to the King, and during these exchanges

[121] On Higdon's career see A. B. Emden, *Biographical Register of the University of Oxford*, ii. 930-1.

[122] York Diocesan Records, Index of Tudor Clergy, s.v. Higdon, shows him in 1529-30 as rector of Pocklington, Stokesley, Kilham, Pickering and Hayton with Bielby. The deanery of York alone was valued in 1535 at £307 per annum (*Valor Eccles.*, v. 1).

[123] Reid, pp. 103, 490.

[124] For John Higdon cf. Emden, *op. cit.*, ii. 931-2.

he assured Cromwell that he would do his utmost in the cause.[125] In January 1536, the treasurer of York reported to Cromwell that Dean Higdon was ill and unlikely to recover; he was willing to resign, if satisfactory arrangements for a pension could be concluded.[126] This illness did not prevent his being to some extent compromised by the Pilgrimage of Grace,[127] and in the event his death did not take place until 5 June 1539.[128] Our two letters illustrate the wide powers exercised by him as Wolsey's deputy. He resolutely refuses to admit an ignorant cleric to a living in Clifford's patronage—an interesting example of reforming zeal in 1520—and he subsequently discusses the internal weaknesses of Bolton and Ferriby, which he undertakes to amend. In relation to these letters it seems important to observe that he was not merely dean of York. In November 1514 he had in fact been appointed vicar general and official of the diocese of York;[129] he writes primarily, we may suppose, in these important judicial and administrative capacities.

Closely connected with Higdon in many public transactions was Archdeacon Thomas Magnus, one of whose letters (no. 19) we print below. It is a neat and beautiful autograph, but lacks intrinsic interest, since the writer merely thanks the Earl for the gift of a fat stag and alludes to the King's recent visit to York. Magnus was nevertheless one of the outstanding Henrician officials of the Tudor North; he can also claim a pre-eminence among its more fabulous ecclesiastical pluralists. A native of Newark and in earlier life a protégé of Archbishop Savage, Magnus took his doctorate at some foreign university and was incorporated at Oxford as late as 1520.[130] His official career shows exceptional length and complexity. He held the archdeaconry of the East Riding from 1504 until his death on 28 August 1550; he was a canon of Windsor from 1520 to 1547 and of Lincoln from 1521 to 1548.[131] At the height of his success in the mid-thirties he was also master of St. Leonard's Hospital at York, master

[125] *L. & P.*, vi. 431; cf. *Lollards and Protestants*, p. 159.

[126] *L. & P.*, x. 84; cf. *ibid.*, 92, 163.

[127] Cf. Reid, pp. 137-8.

[128] His monument in York Minster is now defaced, but for its text see F. Drake, *Eboracum*, p. 496. He founded a fellowship at Brasenose College to be held alternately by a Yorkshireman and a Lincolnshireman.

[129] Emden, *loc. cit.*, cites Reg. Wolsey, York, fos. 3-4; Sede Vacante Reg., York, pt. iii, fo. 592v. Cf. for examples of his work in this capacity *Lollards and Protestants*, pp. 18, 26.

[130] A. Wood, *Fasti Oxonienses*, ed. Bliss, pt. i, c. 53.

[131] Le Neve, *op. cit.*, ii. 135, 198; iii. 143, 392.

of the wealthy college of St. Sepulchre's near York Minster, master of Sibthorpe College, Nottinghamshire, rector of Bedale, Kirkby in Cleveland and Sessay, vicar of Kendal. At this period of his life his eight benefices in the diocese of York alone yielded him £84 per annum.[132] In 1549, when he had resigned some of his promotions, the chantry commissioners for Yorkshire recorded that he was then 86 years of age, his annual stipend from St. Sepulchre's amounting to £43 and the rest of his livings to £572.[133] These weighty emoluments had not, however, been bestowed upon him in vain, since he stood among the most devoted servants of the Tudor dynasty. For a time Magnus was a member of the Privy Council and he participated in at least five diplomatic missions to Scotland between 1516 and 1526; on the one hand he served as treasurer of the wars; on the other, he achieved intimate personal relationships with James V and with Queen Margaret.[134] Like Higdon, Magnus occupied a prominent place on the Duke of Richmond's council. As its surveyor and receiver-general, he undertook the task of ordering its accounts after an initial period of confusion.[135] He played an even more important part than Higdon in subjugating the Northern Convocation to the royal claims. In 1531 he impelled the clergy of the province to grant £18,840 in order to escape the threat of Praemunire, while two years later he rejoiced to hear that Rowland Lee was coming to York to help him handle the matter of the Divorce.[136] Already in this letter he complained that his 'oolde body is nowe soe ofte clogged with infirmitie and unweildenes', and he had already founded by deed a free school and song school at Newark.[137] Nevertheless, many years still stretched before him, and the rest of his journey seems to have carried him into an uncongenial world. A convinced Henrician, he obviously had little in common with the Edwardian protestants. When at last his will came to be proved, it contained the provision, now rendered obsolete by law, that a chantry should be founded to pray for the souls of his father, mother and sisters. He also willed, if he died in York, to be buried 'as con-

[132] On his benefices see A. Hamilton Thompson in *Y.A.J.*, xxiv. 243 n. 4; cf. also *ibid.*, xiv. 410.

[133] *Yorks. Chantry Surveys* (*Surtees Soc.*, xcii), p. 428.

[134] *D.N.B.* has an outline of his diplomatic career.

[135] Reid, pp. 103, 105.

[136] Brit. Mus. Cotton Cleop., E.vi, fo. 257; cf. *Lollards and Protestants*, pp. 155, 159.

[137] *D.N.B.*

venientlie may be to the tombe of my lord Savage, who was my singler good lorde and maister'. After bequests to his parish priests at Bedale and Sessay he completed a not inconsiderable tale of good works by leaving the residue of his property to charitable purposes.[138] Yet in the event, he lies not beside Savage's superb tomb in the choir of York Minster, but under a fine brass of his own in the chancel at Sessay.

Our remaining letters derive almost entirely from members of the northern noble houses, and among them a certain pre-eminence of interest may be claimed for those of the Percies. The stories of the fifth and sixth Earls of Northumberland have long been familiar in outline, yet here they must be viewed in the light of recent research.[139] From the advent of the Tudors, the Percies seemed destined to tragedy, for so vast an agglomeration of northern lands and liberties, such wide-spread tenurial and sentimental loyalties as they inherited, were scarcely compatible with the unitary Tudor state. As their services gradually became less vital to northern administration, a policy of control and ultimately of attrition was applied to them by Wolsey and by Cromwell. Star Chamber fines and the burdens of ambassadorial and Border services seriously embarrassed the fifth Earl, yet the formerly accepted notion that he died in 1527 leaving enormous debts has now been discounted.[140] His son-in-law Cumberland and Dean Higdon reported that he had left only twenty marks in ready cash, but temporary shortages were not uncommon in noble households, and plate worth no less than £666 was subsequently pledged to the abbot of St. Mary's, York, to meet the funeral expenses and the wages of the household.[141] In this same year 1527 the young sixth Earl told a bosom friend, Sir Thomas Arundel, that his father's debts and his own together amounted to 6000 marks,[142] a large sum, yet equivalent only to one year's income of the Percy estates.[143]

Though the fifth Earl, as we shall observe, espoused the Cardinal's cause against the Duke of Norfolk, this did not save his heir from

[138] *Y.A.J.*, xiv. 410, n. 62; Reg. Holgate, fos. 95v-96v.

[139] The basic narrative is in E. B. de Fonblanque, *Annals of the House of Percy*, i, ch. viii, ix, largely followed by G. Brenan, *Hist. of the House of Percy*, i, ch. vi-viii. On the fall of the Percies see Reid, pp. 115-35; M. E. James in *Surtees Soc.*, clxiii, pp. xiv-xvi, and the work of J. M. W. Bean as cited *infra*. For some evidence on the fifth Earl's loyalty see the present editor in *Archaeological Journal*, cxii. 95 *seqq*.

[140] Cf. J. M. W. Bean, *The Estates of the Percy Family, 1416-1537*, p. 142.

[141] *L. & P.*, iv(2). 3134, 3184.

[142] Fonblanque, *op. cit.*, i. 381.

[143] Bean, *op. cit.*, p. 155.

some heavy-handed treatment, since Wolsey, who had educated the young man in his own household, at once assumed his charge incompetent to undertake onerous responsibility. He began by forbidding the new Earl to attend his father's funeral and proceeded to treat the Percy household almost as that of a man attainted.[144] Both before and after this ignominious accession, the sixth Earl's short life seemed beset by every species of misfortune and malignity. He was bullied by Wolsey, repressed by his father, worn by constant ill-health, thwarted in his love for Anne Boleyn,[145] cheated by his rascally favourites, at loggerheads with his brothers and linked in a mockery of marriage with the neurotic and vengeful Mary Talbot, daughter of the fourth Earl of Shrewsbury. Yet in no small degree his troubles also sprang from his own gullibility. His unparalleled alienations of the Percy estates between 1529 and 1531 cannot be explained by the pressure of debt. In many cases these ostensible sales prove to have been gifts to favourites and friends like Sir Reynold Carnaby, Sir Thomas Wharton, Sir Thomas Arundel and Lord Montague.[146] By far the largest of his debts—a sum exceeding £8000—arose from his unwisdom in standing surety for the London financier Antonio Bonvisi. When in 1531 Bonvisi failed to meet his obligations to the crown, the latter was hence able to begin its incursions by taking over the Percy estates in Cumberland.[147] Thereafter this pressure, at first partial and tentative, steadily developed into a policy of liquidation. Sick, dispirited, knowing he would remain childless, alienated from his brother and heir Sir Thomas Percy, filled with a sense of devotion to the King, Northumberland needed little pressure to bring him to complete surrender. Early in 1536 he announced his intention to make the King his heir[148] and in May 1537, less than two months before he died, he agreed upon an immediate transfer of all his estates to the crown, apparently in return for a pension of £1000 a year and a grant of £1000 to meet his debts.[149]

[144] *L. & P., loc. cit.*

[145] The basic narrative is that of Cavendish (*Early Eng. Text Soc.*, ccxliii. 29-34), who was an eyewitness of the interviews between Wolsey and young Percy, and between the latter and his father. Cf. also Fonblanque, *op. cit.*, i. 363 *seqq.*

[146] Bean, *op. cit.*, pp. 145-50. In addition he leased many valuable properties at nominal rents. Cf. for Robert Southwell's contemporary estimate of the position *L. & P.*, xii(2). 548.

[147] Bean, *op. cit.*, p. 156.

[148] The letters are printed by Fonblanque, *op. cit.*, i. 469-471.

[149] *L. & P.*, viii. 166, 363; xii(1). 1121, 1304; xii(2). 19; 27 Hen. VIII cap. 47. On the dating cf. Bean, *op. cit.*, pp. 153-4.

On the other hand, the young Earl has left some evidence of more positive characteristics, which under less tragic circumstances might have enabled him to play an important rôle in the history of the Tudor north. His critics have too often overlooked his zeal for justice and the considerable success with which he adapted himself to the rough and laborious tasks of Border warfare and administration. Seen against the background of a society which grossly overvalued business acumen and material acquisitions, this guileless, kindly and rather muddled young man cannot but attract a measure of sympathy. Amid a generation of nobility and gentry which made a religion of land-investment, the 'unthrifty' Earl achieved at least a refreshing eccentricity. On the other hand, such a tragedy may blind us to the needs and mission of the crown. When Wolsey and his successors sought to undermine the Percy affinity and to win over the northern families by fees and leases, their policy stood ultimately to benefit the nation, since they were crushing not merely individuals but the forces of bastard feudalism and anarchy. Though the dying Earl stood aloof from the Pilgrimage of Grace, his brothers and his servants figured among its chief instigators and leaders.[150] The Hotspur tradition of revolt died hard, and even in the next generation a revived Percy interest was to take the lead in the rising of the Northern Earls. In that world of balladry, lordship and long memories, men proved slow to understand the claims of the nation-state, and the name of Percy, whatever the innocence of its chief bearer, could still threaten a reversion to social and political chaos.

Of the five Percy letters, the one from the 'Magnificent' fifth Earl (no. 30) is a cordial note to his son-in-law Cumberland urging the latter to sell him oaks for repairs to the hall of Cockermouth Castle. The shortage of large timber here mentioned can easily be paralleled in more populous areas of the Tudor north, but it has a special interest at this early date in Cumberland. The fifth Earl died not long after writing this letter, and even if it stood alone it would discourage the suggestion that his financial situation had become desperate. He was not so oppressed by a sense of poverty as to spare considerable expenditure on the hall of a castle in which he seldom resided.

The sixth Earl's letters are all delightfully in character. Perhaps the most important of the four is no. 31, written in October 1526 to the first Earl of Cumberland. The latter had sent his brother-in-law

[150] Reid, pp. 133-5.

many venison pasties to distribute to the Cardinal and others: pleasantly mixing the serious facts with an account of this distribution, the younger Percy describes an extraordinary interview between his own father and Wolsey, during which the fifth Earl urged the Cardinal to put no trust in Cumberland as being 'all with my lord of Norfolk'. Percy then adjures Cumberland to keep this information secret and to be very wary of his actions. If the Earl should mean to do Cumberland any harm, Percy would immediately send further warning. Coming from a naturally mild young man, this letter indicates the depth and permanence of the cleavage between Northumberland and his son. It also shows that an open feud already existed between Wolsey and Norfolk, and that Northumberland, for all his former difficulties with the government, remained to the last a Wolseian. In his final paragraph young Percy gives the latest London news: the attack by the Colonna faction on the Vatican and the King's visit to York Place, where he had 'marvelous high cheer'. In view of his subsequent attitude to Henry VIII, it is tempting to suppose that his devotion to the King, which was to produce such sensational results, had a perfectly genuine and heartfelt character; moreover, that it may have sprung from Henry's personal magnetism and his kindness to Percy during these visits to Wolsey's household.

Percy's other letters were written after his accession to the earldom, and they shed a brief but welcome radiance across his otherwise gloomy biography. In letter 32 he bids his sister and Cumberland to visit the Dacres at Morpeth, 'that we may make mery to geder' at Shrovetide. As indicated below, something more serious than merry-making seems to have taken place at this unusual house-party. Letter 34 was probably written at a serious juncture in the summer of 1532, when Percy had been summoned to London by the King and called upon to explain the nature of his early relations with Anne Boleyn. Here he assures the Cumberlands of the solace their friendship brings him in this troubled world, and tells them that, the King excepted, they are the persons in the world he would fainest see, and in whom 'my most comfort doth rest'. In this mention of the King, it is tempting to detect a merely prudential aside, but in view of the whole evidence we should here probably fall into anachronism and simplification. It is one of the unquestionable, if surprising, facts of the age that Henry VIII inspired love as well as fear. Regarding the sixth Earl's close tie with the Cliffords, the key to the situation evidently lay with his sister, whom he protests that he regards above all other women. Hence the biographer of the Percies may have been unduly lugubrious in describing the Earl's love for Anne Boleyn as 'the one gleam of sunshine that ever brightened the sad life now recorded'.[151] His latest letter here (no. 33) has an official character; he sends Cumberland the royal orders for the provision of a Border contingent, urges him to obey with alacrity, assuages his fear of incurring expense and keeps him abreast of the warlike preparations concerted by himself, Dacre and Wharton.

The three Dacre letters (nos. 26, 27, 28) can scarcely boast this personal and political interest. The Percies were a predominantly Yorkshire family with nation-wide interests and strong connections with the court and the south, but the Dacres remained essentially Border chieftains.[152] Of their activities in this limited sphere, the statepapers contain such ample evidence as to deprive our three letters of anything more than a subsidiary interest. Thomas, second Lord Dacre of Gilsland, who wrote letter 26, was the baron who raised this ancient but hitherto poor family to a much enhanced territorial status by his marriage with the heiress Elizabeth Greystoke. Modern historians are perhaps most deeply indebted to him for dictating in November 1513 an account of a border foray[153] which could be converted with little effort to the needs of a historical novelist. As will appear below,[154] this same account probably dates no. 26, the place of which in the Dacre-Clifford feud has already attracted our notice.[155]

Thomas Lord Dacre died in October 1525 and was succeeded by his son William, who maintained the border traditions of his ancestors, survived the dangerous treason-charges of 1534 and died only six years before the revolt of 1569 and the consequent attainder of his sons. One of his two letters below (no. 27) is directed not to Cumberland but to Sir William Parr, chamberlain to the Duke of Richmond. It states that Wolsey has commanded Dacre to deliver the city and castle of Carlisle to the Bishop of Carlisle to the use of the Earl of Cumberland: hence, no doubt, the preservation of this letter in the Clifford archives, since the delivery had become a matter of dispute.[156] Another clash between the families is recalled by Dacre's

[151] Fonblanque, *op. cit.*, i. 373.
[152] Cf. Reid, p. 93.
[153] Printed in H. Ellis, *Original Letters, first series*, i. 93-9.
[154] *Infra*, p. 97.
[155] *Supra*, p. 30.
[156] *L. & P.*, iv(1). 1762.

letter 28, which recalls that the President and Council in the North have made a 'raykenyng and ordre' between them, and asks Cumberland for a money-payment due under this order. During the less bitter periods, these magnates seem to have attempted to preserve at least a decent civility; Dacre here writes half-apologetically and says he is compelled to 'muster money' in order to go up to London.

No less than nine of our items come from the Scropes of Bolton, whose magnificent castle so fascinated the heavy Leland[157] and still, with its added memories of Mary Stuart, dominates the bleak uplands of Wensleydale. The earliest of these writers was Henry, the seventh baron, who figures in the Elizabethan ballad of Flodden:

> 'With lusty lads and large of length
> Which dwelt on Semerwaterside,
> All Richmondshire its total strength
> The valiant Scrope did lead and guide.'

Born about 1480, he had succeeded his father in 1506; he served once more against the Scots in 1522 and died about December 1533.[158] We have already noticed his request (no. 37) for payment of the hundred pounds due to him under the terms of the marriage between his son and Cumberland's eldest daughter Lady Katherine Clifford. He also wrote to the Earl (no. 38) on behalf of Anne Wibergh, a servant of his wife dispossessed of her lands by one Thomas Wibergh; 'which I suppose doth belonge to youre Lordshyppe'. Below, we show in detail that these persons were in fact husband and wife, and that Anne's family, the Lowthers, waged a series of quarrels with the Wiberghs, then an almost equally well-known Westmorland family. This letter serves to indicate that when the heads of the great noble houses were sensible, they came together to solve disputes between their satellites; under the watchful eye of Tudor government, the once chaotic system of affinities could have a law-keeping as well as a law-breaking function.

John, eighth Lord Scrope, is said to have married Katherine Clifford about 1530, though the Earl's accounts for 1525 already show a payment of £2 13s. 4d. to the papal collector for a licence

[157] *Itineraries*, ed. L. Toulmin Smith, v. 139-40.

[158] G.E.C., xi. 546-7. For his inscription and that of his sons in Wensley church see T. D. Whitaker, *Richmondshire*, i. 373-4; H. B. McCall, *Richmondshire Churches*, pp. 167, 174. For a good pedigree see N. H. Nicolas, *The Controversy between Sir Richard Scrope and Sir Robert Grosvenor*, ii. 61-2.

of marriage between the pair, who were then children.[159] John subsequently held various northern offices and stewardships, took a thirty years' lease of the dissolved abbey of St. Agatha, Easby, and was an executor under the will of his father-in-law Cumberland. He then served as a Warden of the West March from 1542 to 1547, conducted Scottish prisoners to York after Solway Moss, went by sea with Hertford in the Scottish expedition of 1544 and died five years later.[160] Two of his letters (nos. 40, 41), referring to the involved disputes between himself and Sir Christopher Metcalfe, have already received mention[161] and are discussed in more detail below. Letter 42 he appears to have written shortly before his father's death, and here he urges his father-in-law Cumberland to use his influence upon the course of a suit concerning the 'wardship of Thursby', probably meaning that of William Thoresby of Thoresby in Aysgarth. In this dispute the antagonist of the Scropes was the feodary Edmund Copendale, while the chief member of the commission of enquiry due to sit at Thirsk was Sir Robert Bowes. In young Scrope's view, even Bowes appeared far from impartial, and he now begs Cumberland to warn both Copendale and Bowes not to be 'so extreyme and parshall' against his father's cause, 'with sum quyck clawsys of your Lordshipes mynd, as ye thinke good'.

At the outset of the Pilgrimage of Grace, John Lord Scrope found himself among those many of the gentry who feared to participate, but who were nevertheless compelled by the commons to accompany them in their march. On Thursday 12 October 1536 he wrote to Cumberland that the commons of Masham and Nidderdale had risen the previous day, had occupied Coverham Abbey and Middleton, and were now advancing on Bolton Castle to capture him. He had therefore left his wife and house and intended to stay abroad till he knew the purpose of the rebels. He also begged Cumberland to send back advice to his wife Katherine, Cumberland's daughter.[162] As ill-luck would have it, he failed to evade the rebels, and some time before

[159] *Craven*, p. 33. In 1523-4 there had been long but fruitless negotiations aimed at a marriage between John and Katherine Parr, later Lady Latimer and ultimately Queen of England. The interesting correspondence on this subject between his grandfather Lord Dacre and Katherine's mother Lady Maud Parr, is printed in Whitaker, *Richmondshire*, i. 384-8.

[160] G.E.C., xi. 547-8. For a description of his portrait, formerly at Bolton Hall, see Whitaker, *op. cit.*, i. 383.

[161] *Supra*, p. 34.

[162] *L. & P.*, xi. 677

17 October was forcibly sworn to accompany them.[163] These facts were already known, but we did not know where he attempted to hide and, a more interesting matter, what happened to Katherine. Doubtless well-known by the rebels as a daughter of the hated Earl, she was left stranded at Bolton over thirty miles from her father's besieged castle at Skipton. Now these questions are answered by letter 35, certainly the most 'romantic' item of our collection. Katherine wrote it in her own hand to her father before daybreak on Saturday, 14 October; its clarity and determination seem all the more admirable in that she had a baby to keep from the clutches of the hostage-seeking insurgents and was probably little more than nineteen years of age. She began with the most lucid extant account of the movements of the Richmondshire commons, who had divided themselves into three parties in order to seize the gentry; one moving up Wensleydale for the Scropes, Metcalfes and Siggiswicks, another seeking Lord Latimer at Snape and Sir Christopher Danby at Thorpe Perrow, the third marching on Barnard Castle for George Bowes and his uncles. Her husband Lord Scrope lay that night at Helbeck Hall, near Brough under Stainmore,[164] but planned to ride south for Skipton, 'to take suche parte as your Lordship dothe'. Katherine had sent her 'little boy',[165] with his nurse to hide in a poor man's house and she herself planned to ride that morning toward Kettlewell, some sixteen miles from Bolton and almost half-way toward Skipton. There she would be in a position not merely to rejoin her husband, but to await her father's instructions, sent back to Kettlewell by the present messenger. This may be commended as a most sensible plan; she surmised that an obscure messenger might easily get through to her father, or at least return with a clear picture of the situation around Skipton. And she did not fail in the stress of the moment to conclude in the stately phrases demanded of a young noblewoman to her parents: 'Thus tholy Gost preserve your good Lordship with my Lady my mother and all youres in comfort.' To avoid a confusion likely to beset readers unfamiliar with the Pennine country, it may here be added that these events have no ostensible connection with the famous rescue of the other Clifford ladies by Christopher, brother

[163] *L. & P.*, xi. 759; cf. Dodds, i. 208.

[164] This house belonged to Thomas Blenkinsop, a gentleman of old family and a close associate of the Cliffords (Nicholson and Burn, i. 584).

[165] Probably Henry, the future ninth Baron Scrope, b. 1534. She had an older son, who d. very early, probably before this date, since she mentions only the one child.

of Robert Aske.[166] Katherine's sister-in-law the Lady Eleanor Clifford (*née* Brandon) and two others of Cumberland's daughters were then at Bolton *Priory,* only six miles east of Skipton and over thirty miles distant, across rough country, from Katherine's home at Bolton Castle. It was the week after Katherine wrote this letter that Christopher Aske smuggled these ladies through the besiegers into the safety of Skipton Castle. Katherine's later movements are admittedly unrecorded, and it is just possible that, having reached Kettlewell, she turned aside to join her sisters at Bolton Priory, and hence to be rescued by Aske. But we have no information to suggest such an event, and Cumberland had three younger daughters,[167] two of whom are far more likely than Katherine to have been present at the Priory with the Lady Eleanor.

Curiously and fortunately, we have here a second letter (no. 36) by Katherine, written nearly half a century later to her great-nephew the third Earl of Cumberland. The setting is Elizabethan and the other *dramatis personae* are all children of the new age. After Scrope's death she had married, as his second wife, Sir Richard Cholmeley, 'the great black knight of the North'.[168] She bore him children and endured his infidelities, but after his death in May 1583 she used her former name Katherine Scrope. By his first wife Sir Richard had a son Francis, who succeeded to the principal Cholmeley estates, but 'died about Pentecost, anno 1586, sans issue'.[169] On 20 June 1583, 1584 or 1585, Katherine wrote this letter concerning the commission appointed to adjudicate between Francis Cholmeley and, on the other hand, herself, her own son Henry Cholmeley and her son-in-law Richard Dutton. In the event, this settlement was made, yet proved of short duration. When Francis died childless, he was succeeded by Henry, since the late Sir Richard Cholmeley had executed a deed of entail giving Henry preference over two other sons by his first wife.[170] As for Katherine, she survived until 1598, spending her last years with her son Henry at Whitby. She had become a convinced Roman Catholic and she heads the list of Whitby recusants in the York archiepiscopal visitation book of 1590: *Domina*

[166] Cf. *supra*, p. 24.

[167] Maud, Elizabeth and Jane. Cf. *infra*, pp. 139-40.

[168] For his biography see *Parliamentary Representation of the Co. of York* (*Y.A.S. Rec. Ser.*, xcvi), ed. A. Gooder, ii. 17-19.

[169] *Glover's Visitation*, p. 220.

[170] G. Young, *Hist. Whitby*, ii. 829-30.

Katherina Scropp, vidua.[171] We can only regret that she did not belong to a generation when ladies wrote their memoirs. From her early childhood she perhaps remembered her grandfather the Shepherd Lord, whose own memories stretched back well into the Wars of the Roses. In 1598 she could have told anecdotes of the canons of Bolton to children like her grand-niece Anne Clifford, who knew Restoration England. And by her last years must she not have been the only great lady capable of stirring reminiscences about her adventures in the Pilgrimage of Grace?

The remainder of the letters we select for special comment were also written by women. Katherine's sister Lady Maud Clifford married John, third Lord Conyers of Hornby and Skelton in Cleveland. At the death of his father Christopher on 14 June 1538, this young nobleman was barely fifteen years of age, but indentures for the marriage had already been drawn up by his parents and the first Earl of Cumberland. Two days after his father's death, his mother wrote an acquittance to the Earl (no. 24) acknowledging the receipt of 100 marks, half the sum payable by the Earl under these indentures. This widow, Anne Lady Conyers, was a daughter of Thomas Lord Dacre of Gilsland. Her will, dated 16 December 1547, describes her as 'dowager of Skelton'; its provisions indicate completely orthodox Catholic belief and stipulate that she shall be buried at All Saints', Skelton, 'In the tombe beside my lorde, my husbande'.[172] Here the markedly affectionate references to her son harmonise with her letter (no. 25) printed below. It is merely dated 'the present Goodfryday', but may confidently be placed either in 1539 or, with less likelihood, in 1540. She describes to the first Earl of Cumberland an interview with Thomas Cromwell, Lord Privy Seal, who had 'very gently' accepted her son and promised to place him in the King's service. At the same time, Lady Conyers asks that her daughter-in-law Maud Clifford may stay for the time being with the Earl. The young couple were presumably not yet cohabiting, and in her straitened circumstances Lady Conyers cannot have been eager to maintain the girl and her attendants. A letter by her in the state-papers is dated 17 October 1539 and it tells Cromwell that since the death of her husband she and her children have been compelled to live on loans from their friends. Her husband's creditors have called

[171] Cf. the present editor in *Y.A.J.*, xxxv. 176-7.

[172] *Test. Ebor.*, vi. 263-4, proved 21 April 1548. What is probably the matrix of the second Lord Conyers' brass remains in Skelton church (*Y.A.J.*, xxii. 387n.).

upon her to pay debts which she could only settle when in control of the rents assigned to that purpose by the late Lord Conyers. She begs Cromwell to take no displeasure at her incessant clamour, since she is constrained to it by extreme poverty.[173] The minister, who often acted as money-lender to impoverished notables, advanced in all about £131 to the young Lord Conyers in the early months of 1539.[174]

The sad little note from the Countess Eleanor to her husband (no. 44) tells its own story: 'Jesu send hus both healthe'. This devoted pair had been given so many of the world's gifts and denied the one most precious. In frank detail she describes her symptoms—on which we subjoin a medical note—and asks the Earl to send in all haste her favourite physician 'Doctor Stephyns', perhaps that same Stephen Thomson of York who in earlier years had tended the sixth Earl of Northumberland.[175]

Finally, we should draw attention to the tragi-comic letter (no. 23) written by Anne Clifton, a married daughter of the Shepherd Lord, to her brother, later the first Earl. In decisive terms she upbraids Sir Harry for failing to help her in her troubles. This repetitive and rather incoherent autograph forms a piquant social and human document, for it represents almost precisely what a Tudor lady might say in angry *viva voce* argument with a neglectful male relative. Not long beforehand Anne had married, as a second wife, Robert Clifton, the head of a well-known Nottinghamshire family with houses and estates at Hodsock, in Blyth parish, and at Clifton near Nottingham, where its memorials may still be seen in the church.[176] In September 1517 Robert died, leaving Anne with her baby Gervase still under two years of age and with a daughter.[177] Like Lady Conyers in later years, she had at the time of writing been prevented from drawing income from her husband's lands since his death. In addition, she was beset by his grasping relatives, who sought to turn her out of her houses. It was no small wonder that she waxed indignant on learning that her brother, although in London, had not interceded with Wolsey and other influential officials on her behalf. Yet we may well think of her as relying upon a broken reed, when we recall that

[173] *L. & P.*, xiv(2). 344. For a description of the lands in the hands of the crown by reason of this minority see P.R.O., Ministers' Accounts, Hen. VIII, 4281.

[174] *L. & P.*, xiv(2). 782, pp. 325, 335, 340.

[175] On this identification and an alternative cf. *infra*, pp. 125-6.

[176] On the Cliftons see Thoroton, *Hist. Nottinghamshire*, ed. Throsby, i. 104; A. C. Wood in *Thoroton Soc.*, xxxvii. 34; *Test. Ebor.*, iv. 64-71, 276-7.

[177] Dorothy Clifton, mentioned in the first Earl's will (*Y.A.J.*, xviii. 376).

the future Earl, still wild and aggressive, had a few months earlier been imprisoned by Wolsey and the Council. One wonders why their father, the now elderly Shepherd Lord, had taken no effective steps to aid his daughter.[178] Perhaps he stood on bad terms with her, as well as with Sir Harry Clifford, but it seems more likely that amid the wooded solitudes of Barden, his mind set on alchemy and the Carthusians, he had already become lethargic and insensitive to all the problems of his offspring. Here is but one of the many relationships between our characters upon which we could wish the letters threw a more searching light. Students of Tudor society will not lack appreciation for new sources with so lively a human interest, yet at every point our fresh insights pose new questions, stress our ignorance and stimulate our curiosity concerning a generation so like and yet so unlike our own. In the last resort we are tempted to regard these Tudor people as essentially inarticulate. Their silences remain profound, and they leave us ample freedom to wield the fascinating but dangerous weapons of imaginative reconstruction.

[178] She is said by Lady Anne Clifford to have married Robert Metcalfe, but this tradition is beset by difficulties. Cf. *infra*, p. 131.

1

The Abbot and Convent of Byland to the first Earl of Cumberland, [*Undated; c.* 1525-1526]

See introduction, p. 31. This letter must have been written under the last abbot of Byland, John Ledes, *alias* Alanbridge, who was elected in March 1525 (Dugdale, v. 345). The reference to the breaking of the seal of the former abbot implies a date shortly after Ledes' election. Bleatarn is a hamlet in the parish of Warcop, Westmorland, and the manor, given to Byland in the reign of Henry II, remained in its hands to the dissolution; a cell had been founded there, the ruins of which survived to the eighteenth century (Nicholson & Burn, i. 614-16; D. Scott, *Cumberland and Westmorland*, pp. 193-4). Byland had received gifts of land in Warcop from at least six donors (J. Burton, *Monasticon Eboracense*, p. 337) and the Ministers' Accounts value them at £20 annually (Dugdale, v. 355). Abbot Ledes received an annual pension of £50 and was still alive during the pensions-enquiry of 1553 (Exch. K. R. Accts. bdle 76, no. 24). For further particulars concerning him, cf. G. R. Elton, *Star Chamber Stories*, pp. 152-67 *passim*, 231, nn. 22, 24; *Yorks. Star Chamber Proceedings*, i (*Y.A.S. Rec. Ser.*, xli), pp. 48-51.

This letter is not signed by the abbot; it is couched in the first person plural and subscribed in the same hand as the body of the letter.

(fo. 1)

In owr moste humble maner we recommende us unto yowr good Lordisshipe, signifiyng unto youe that we, yowr fathfull & true orators, haith receved yowr moste lovyng and kynde lettres, wherin we doe perceve that your good Lordesshipe doith not entend to exclude and put us frome the occupacion off owr londes of Blat[ar]ne & Warcope & reentre thereunto, for the more profeet of owr poer hows, a yeir before the terme of yowr lease, onlesse ye doe compounde with us for the rennyng of the same. Yff it like yowr Lordisshipe to understonde (no disp[l]easure taken) the leasse is cassat, voyd and of none effecte, for the seale of owr predecessor is broken & put away, & also he hade none autorite to make ony leasse but duryng is lyffe naturall. Wherfore iff it wolde please yowr Lordisshipe to be contented as to suffre yowr humble bedmen & daily orators soner to make entry to the said londes, then you dide expresse in yowr moste discret lettres, we shall fathfully admit you and my Lady yowr wyff with all yowr noble yssue to be brethren & sisters off owr chapitor and to be partinars of all owr spirituall suffrages, and not only this, but also we shall be contented to doe unto yowr Lordisshipe a pleasure, with the grace of Gode, who have yowr moste noble Lordisshipe with all yowr progeny in his everlasting tuicion. Frome Biland,

By yowr assured daily
orators, thabbot & covent of the same.

[Endorsed, fo. 1v)] To the ryght honorable and worshipefull the Lorde off Commerlande.

2

Lancelot, Prior of Carlisle, to the first Earl of Cumberland, 24 *November* [1537]

See introduction, p. 31. The year is supplied by the reference to 'the commotion', i.e. the Pilgrimage. On 17 December 1534, the Earl had written that he possessed the 'tithe corns' of Kirkland, Cumberland, by force of a dimission made to him by the prior at the King's request (*L. & P.*, vii. 1549). Lancelot Salkeld, last prior and first dean of Carlisle, resigned the deanery under Edward VI, was restored under Mary, subscribed to the Elizabethan Settlement, and died in office, 3 September 1560 (*V.C.H.*, *Cumberland*, ii. 58-65 gives references).

Signed.

(fo. 2)

Ryght honorabill and my most synguler gud Lorde, pleasitt your gud Lordshipe too be advertyshitt that I desyre your gud Lordshipe for Christe sayke that ye wilbe soo gud Lord unto me as to content and pay me the half yere rent off the teithe of Kyrklond, whiche is awynge me. Yff your Lordship wold call too your remembrance, ye did pay unto my supprior the Thurseday before Our Lady day in Lent[1] after the commotion x^{li} x^{s} for the half yere rent[2] whiche was

[1] Thursday 22 March 1537.
[2] 'Rent' interpolated.

dewe unto me at Saincte Andrewe day[3] before, as doith appeyre by your acquytance, the whiche your Lordship did receyve by the handes of the said supprior; and thother half yere rentt, whiche shuld have bein pait too me at the Invention off the Cross,[4] I had none for that half yere, as I will answere God Almyghty God [*sic*] upon the day of jugement. The premisses consyderit, I trust that ye will be gud Lord unto me, as your Lordship haith beine before tyme. I am lothe to dysplease your gud Lordship, as knawith Almyghty God, who have you alway in his most blyssid tuycion. Att Carliell, this xxiiij day of Novembre, by your dayly orator and beidman at his litill power,

Lancelot, prior
off the same.

[Endorsed, fo. 2v] Too his ryght honorabyll and most synguler gud Lord, my Lord Erle off Cumberland, dylyver this with [*blank*].

3

The Prior and Convent of Furness to the first Earl of Cumberland,
10 *June* [?1531]

See introduction, p. 30. The Earl having requested a lease of the Abbey's manor of Winterburn (in Gargrave, 4½ miles N.W. of Skipton), the prior and convent here ask for a respite of over three months to take outside advice, on the ground that they are merely 'the bodie of the convent'. This strongly suggests that at the time the house had no abbot. The only possible vacancy to which the remark could refer occurred in 1531, when Alexander Banks died and was succeeded by Roger Pele, the last abbot. Despite the contradictory dates given in works of reference, there can be little doubt that Pele succeeded in 1531, since he then paid £200 for his admission and confirmation (*L. & P.*, v. 657; cf. *ibid.*, 849). Our letter thus forms the initial stage of Cumberland's long struggle to gain and keep control over the Winterburn lands, a major source of revenue estimated by a rental of 1535 at £51-12-6 (T. A. Beck, *Annales Furnesienses*, p. 330). On the death of Abbot Banks, a monk named

[3] 30 November 1536, when the Pilgrimage was at its height.
[4] 3 May 1537.

Hugh Brown robbed his bedroom, broke open the chest containing the common seal, and sealed blank parchments, upon which leases were afterwards made of Winterburn and other Yorkshire lands to the Earl of Cumberland (*V.C.H., Lancs.*, ii. 123; Beck, *op. cit.*, App. ix, pp. lxxxvii *seqq.*). In June 1533 Abbot Pele sought Cromwell's protection against Cumberland's pressures. Cf. *L.* & *P.*, vi. 632; the letter is quoted by Beck, *op. cit.*, p. 340, but he is probably mistaken in dating it 1535. In 1534 John Proctor complained in the Star Chamber that Cumberland's servants had expelled him from Furness lands in Winterburn leased by him; moreover they had imprisoned him for two months in Skipton Castle. Cf. *Yorks. Star Chamber Proceedings*, iv (*Y.A.S. Rec. Ser.*, lxx), pp. 52-3. The Earl nevertheless managed to retain *de facto* control. In July 1537 Robert Southwell wrote to Cromwell that the tenants of Winterburn were complaining against Cumberland. The manor was 'replenisshide wyth tall men, and in value L. li by the yere or above, wher as my seide Lorde wolde have it for xxxii li by the yere' (Beck, *op. cit.*, p. 359; *L.* & *P.*, xii(2). 206). When Southwell had exposed the invalidity of the Earl's lease, Cumberland admitted as much to Cromwell, but claimed that he had already received Cromwell's permission, confirmed under seal of the Court of Augmentations, to keep the land in farm for the term of the lease (*L.* & *P.*, xii(2). 279). Meanwhile in 1536 there developed a dispute between Cumberland and the Earl of Derby over the stewardship of Winterburn; for this, see letter 43 *infra*. Finally, a group of plaintiffs claiming prior leases challenged the Earl both in the Star Chamber and in the Court of Augmentations (1542), and the unsavoury story of Hugh Brown's misdeeds was told in both courts. For extracts from these depositions, see Beck, *op. cit.*, App. ix, pp. lxxxvii *seqq.*; for the undated, but probably earlier, Star Chamber suit, see *Yorks. Star Chamber Proceedings*, iv (*Y.A.S. Rec. Ser.*, lxx), pp. 136-8.

Mr. Roger Tempest resided at Broughton, 3 miles W. of Skipton (pedigree in *Craven*, p. 106). 'Mr. Berie' is probably the priest William Berie, who appears as an executor of the Earl's will and as 'Mr. William Berie', in the codicil (*Y.A.J.*, xviii. 379); he was also an important witness in the Augmentations suit of 1542 (Beck, *op. cit.*, App. ix, p. xci). A priest of this name was vicar of Kirkby in Cleveland in 1554 and of Gilling in 1557 (York Diocesan Records, Index of Tudor Clergy, s.v. Bery, Wm.).

This letter is not signed by the prior, but subscribed in the same hand as the body of the letter.

(fo. 3)

Right honorable and oure especiall good Lorde, in oure full humble wyse we commende us to your good Lordshipe. And where we perceyve by your counselors Mr Roger Tempest & Mr Berie that ye be desireous to have one take[5] or lease of oure lordshipe of Winterburne, with apportenance, in this matter we beseche youe to be good lord to us & oure monasterie, and that we may have respite to giffe youre good Lordshipe one answere betwixt this & the feaste of Saynte Michaell tharchangell,[6] for soo myche that we, that ar the bodie of the convent, can gyffe noo direct answere to noo suche mater witheout some good advisement. Suerlye & God, if ony levyng man under oure Prince have the saide Winterburne, withe thapportenance, youre goode Lordshipe shalbe the fyrste. And as we ar and may be youre poore beydmen, that it may please youe to be good lorde unto oure poore monasterie. And so doynge, ye bynde us for ever to be youre daylye orators, as knawithe Oure Lorde, whoo have youe in his blessed tuicion. Frome Forneys the x[t] days of Juny,

Youre humble orators, the
prior & convent of Forneys.

[Endorsed, fo. 3v) To there right honorable and especiall good Lorde, therle of Cumbrelande, delyvered be this.

4

Thomas, Abbot of Holm Cultram, to the first Earl of Cumberland, 30 August [?1534]

See introduction, p. 31. Thomas Ireby had restitution of the temporalities of the house between 22 November 1532 and 11 March 1533 (*L. & P.*, vi. 228); he died 10 August 1536. The indenture to which he refers was almost certainly that transferring to the Earl of Cumberland the stewardship of Holm Cultram, formerly held by William Lord Dacre until his disgrace in May 1534. By the summer of 1535, the Earl had become steward (*Valor Eccles.*, v. 283). Hence the date 30 August 1534 seems appropriate. On the last abbots, and the bad disciplinary state of Holm, see *V.C.H., Cumberland*, ii. 170-73.

Signed.

[5] A lease of land or of a farm for a term of years. Cf. examples of 1511 and 1542 in *Test. Ebor.*, v. 24; vi. 157.

[6] 29 Sept.

(fo. 4)

My Lord, my dewtey reservyt, I recommend me onto yow, certefyng yow we have resavyt the Kynges Grace letter, & accordyng to the said letter we schall maik one indenture & to delyveryt onto your Lordschyp when ye come in to the contre. And yf ye think yt be not to the Kynges Grace letter & your plesure, ye schall cawse your secretore to mayk yt accordyn onto the indenture that Wylliam Lord Dacre had, & this yow schall have with our dayly prayer & favore. No more to yow at this tyme, but Jhesu kepe yow, Amen. From Abbay Holme, the xxx^{ti} day of August,

By your kynde lovyng beydman,
Thomas, abbot off tholm.

[Endorsed, fo. 4v] To the ryght honorable Lord, the Erle of Comberland, be this d[elivere]d.

5

John [*Norton*], *Prior of Mountgrace, to Lord Clifford,*
27 *August* [?1521].

See introduction, pp. 28, 35-6. The letter, an autograph throughout, is in a hand different from that of Prior John Wilson (nos. 6-9 *infra*); its style also suggests another writer and it may hence be attributed to Wilson's predecessor John Norton, the mystical writer, prior of Mountgrace from 1509-10 to 1521-2. This letter may be placed very near the end of Norton's priorate, because its themes are continuous with those of Wilson's letters. We know that these building activities under Clifford's patronage continued under Prior Wilson (nos. 6, 8 *infra*), while 'Edward your servand' mentioned in this letter was presumably the Edward Exley who also appears as intermediary between Clifford and Wilson in 1523 (no. 7 *infra*).

Autograph.

Jhesus[7] Maria

(fo. 5)

My Lorde, plays it your Lordshippe to onderstand that Goddes warke

[7] MS: 'Ihc'.

and yours gosse wylle forward, lovyd by Godde, as Edward your servand cane showe your Lordshuppe, for, as Godde knawys, I have spende your mony and muche more, as Edward cane reherce to your Lordshuppe, qwatt warkmen I have in every corner. And nowe I muste go by more ledde, for I thynke to have iij sellis thekyt with lede a fore wynter. Also I muste pay for ccxxx wanscottes, of this mony x^{li}, as I have showyd Edward, of qwome I have resavyd at this tym xv^{li} $xiij^{s}$ $iiij^{d}$ in xxvij day of August, to qwome I have showyd all the newys that I have at this tyme. Frome the Monte Grace,

By your bedman John, prior ther.

[No endorsement]

6

John [*Wilson*], *Prior of Mountgrace, to Lord Clifford, Feast of St. Lucy,* 13 *December* [1522]

See introduction, p. 36. With regard to the many pious provisions mentioned in this and the other letters from Prior Wilson, it should be recalled that Lord Clifford was seriously ill by the autumn of 1522 and that he died on 23 April 1523. The writer begins this complicated letter by discussing problems connected with two purchases of land to be made with Clifford's money. The first, in Teesdale, was to support Clifford's anchorage and had been arranged by Prior Norton. The second, apparently a benefaction to Mountgrace itself, was to consist of land in Beswick, 5½ miles N.N.W. of Beverley. Here Mountgrace had made a conditional bargain with the present owner. They had paid the latter £70; if he could repay this money by 1 August 1523, they had agreed to return his deeds, yet this seemed unlikely, since he was an improvident gentleman. If he failed to repay, Mountgrace would then remit him the balance of the purchase-price (£30), and so enter into possession.[8] Prior Wilson had borrowed the £70, and would have to borrow another £21 for the Teesdale purchase, unless Clifford now forwarded the cash. Wilson then alludes to the significant conversation with John, heir of Richard Neville, second Lord Latimer of Snape. John Neville in fact succeeded to the title

[8] The *Valor Eccles.*, v. 84 actually shows Mountgrace in possession of lands at Beswick worth £6 per annum.

in 1530, married Katherine Parr, was involved in the Pilgrimage of Grace, and died in March 1543 (references in *Lollards and Protestants*, pp. 62-3). Again, Wilson gives details of the building operations at Mountgrace, to which a London merchant, recently made a Knight of Rhodes (i.e. a Hospitaller), had contributed. The prior finally invites Clifford to visit Mountgrace (but not before the summer!) and urges him to make sure provision for his benefactions to the house, before anything should happen to him. Though Clifford died four months later, nos. 7 and 8 *infra* were written to him after the present letter: e.g. in no. 8 a later stage of the Teesdale purchase is described. Hence the date 1522 for our present letter. 'Baron Hilton' was Sir William Hilton of Hilton, Durham, whose family, descended from Alexander, second Lord Hilton (d. 1360), continued to style themselves barons of Hilton and were commonly accorded the title by others (*L.* & *P.*, iii(2). 3135, 3395). On this family see G.E.C., vii. 30-32; Clay, p. 106. 'Banbrige of Teisdale' is the 'Alane Banbrige' mentioned in no. 8 *infra*, where further details of this purchase are given. He was probably of the Baynbriggs of Freer House in the parish of Middleton in Teesdale, though their incomplete pedigrees do not include him. The *Valor Eccles.*, v. 84 shows Mountgrace holding lands in Middleton in Teesdale worth £5 per annum, which may have included the present purchase. The other two branches of the family at Snotterton and Wheatly Hill also show no Alan (*Pedigrees . . . of Durham*, ed. J. Foster, pp. 5, 7, 9). For Sir William Malleverer of Woodsome, see *Glover's Visitation*, p. 201. Further connections between this family and Mountgrace appear in no. 7 *infra*. The Fulthorpe family was of Fulthorpe and Tunstall, Durham, and of Hipswell near Richmond. Christopher was aged 20 in 1487 (Surtees, *Durham*, iii. 126). While this seems the most likely identification, there were other branches and other Christophers. Cf. Nicholson and Burn, i. 551.

Autograph. Wilson's hand in this and the three subsequent letters has marked Italianate characteristics.

(fo. 5v blank)
(fo. 6)

Right honorable, and my owne most trusty & hartely biloved goode Lord in our Saveyor Christe Jhesu, I humbely recommend me to your Lordshyp, desyryng your prosperouse helth, both bodely and gostely, to the plesor of God: lettyng your Lordship understond that I must maike a payment shortly of the xx^{s}[9] lande in Teisdaille, wich our father my predecessor purchessed for your angrege, & his commandes to pay xxj li., wich I thynk vere much, albeit thei wold very

[9] 'xx^{s}' interpolated above the line.

gladly have me to releesse, & soo I thought to have done, but it was shewid me by a secrete frende that it is goode land, and that Baron Hilton wold gyve xxij li. for itt. Also the v marke land, the wich I shewid your Lordship of, is holden of the Kyng in capite, & soo I dar not mell[10] therwith, for wee may not porchesse noo such laandes with owt a speciall licence. Neverthelesse, the same gentilman haith vj li. lande in Besswik v mylle from Beverley, for the wich he was profferd xxiiij yere porchesse, but he is sory to selle itt, and soo came to me & said that he must nedes make shifftt for money; and if it war soo that he shuld selle his land, that wee shuld have it be fore any other, for theintent that he may be prayed for. And of this wee have maid a bargan condicionally after this maner: he haith made hus a dede of saile, as strong os we can devyse be our counsell lernyd, & deliverd posession of the same, and I have paid hym iij.^{xx}x li.,[11] and if soo be that he repae this summe be twix this & Sancte Petre day advincula,[12] we to deliver his dedes; & of this he haith bound hym, his heres & his executores, by statute marchand[13] in one c. li., as strongly as we cane devyse. Yff not, we to inyoye the land, payng the rest of money at Michaellmes next folowyng, which comyth to xxx li. Ther is none that knowith hym that thynkith he shalbe able to repae hus, but rather to selle more land, for he is indette & also a grete riator. I assure you, my owne good Lord, I have bowrrowd this lxx li., and must doo the xxj li. which Banbrige of Teisdale shuld have, except that I have soccor frome your Lordshyp shortly. Also Sir John Nevell, my Lord Latymar son & here, was at our place of late, and sumthyng I brak to hym, os your Lordship had a grete mynde to hym & os ye intended to put hym in trust to doo for you. Wherwith, os I did perceave, he was well content & said he haith bene dyverse tymes moved to have come to your Lordship to have comforted you in your goodnes, & to have gyven you thankes for your gret benefettes to hus & our poore house, and said he wold be redy when sumever it pleased your Lordship to come & speke with you, oyther when I cum or any other tyme when your Lordship thynkith best. Also Sir William Maleverey & Mr Christofer Fulthorpe

[10] Meddle; cf. *New Eng. Dict.*, s.v. mell v^2. The word is interpolated.

[11] I.e. three score and ten pounds.

[12] 1 August.

[13] A bond of record, acknowledged before the chief magistrate of a trading town, giving to the obligee power to seize land of the obligor if he failed to pay his debt at the appointed time: these powers were derived from the Statute of Merchants of 1285 (*New. Eng. Dict.* s.v. statute merchant, gives references).

er speciall good frendes to hus. Moreover, my Lord, I thynk ther be as money stones hewen as will fynnych the houses, and I thynk best at the walle that shall[14] goo aboute the gardyn be made ['of' *cancelled*] with archeleres stone, for elles I cannot devyse[15] os it may be made sure. Wherin I wold gladly know your Lordshypes plesor, for peraventor we may gytt masones now better to hew by grete[16] then in sommer. Also I have[17] paid to masones, gitteres[18] of stone, and to ridderes of the qwarrell,[19] xii li., wich I shall make your Lordship profiet too, when your servand comyth to hus. If it plesse your Lordship, I shall come to you affter Cristynmes, & all my bredren wolbe content that I bring our selle for the indentores. Mi Lorde, wee have a propre lodgyng at our place, wich a marchand of London did bulde, & he is now departed frome hus & made knyght at the Roddes. Whe[r]fore, if it wold plesse God & your Lordship, I wold be glad that ye came & see your warke, that wee myght have your counsell therin, & trust it wollde be to you grete comforth and a good recreacion. I am sure your Lordship wold like your lodgeyng well for the tyme, & I shuld make the best shifft that I cuth for your servandes. Now for the love of God, my Lord, make allthynges sure, for your Lordship doith know the unstablenes of this worlde; and if it war soo that ought came to your Lordship but goode, except ye make it sure be fore, ye know we war with owte remedy, therfor os our trust is in your Lordship remembre hus. And I besek your Lordship to take noo displesor that I send thus ofte and bowldly to your Lordship, for I assure you,[20] my Lord, necessite compellith me; wee have[21] soo many matteres lefft nowe & portte soo grette charges, os your Lordship doith know parte;[22] & I have noo soccor but onely you, os knowith Our Lord, who have your good Lordship in his blissed tuicion. At Mountgrace in festo Sancte Lucie Virginis. Mi lorde, I move you not to come to hus be fore summar.

Your faithfull bedman,

John, priour of the same.

[14] 'Shall' interpolated.

[15] 'Devyse' interpolated.

[16] Wholesale; at a fixed price for the whole amount.

[17] 'Have' interpolated.

[18] Getters.

[19] Cf. the accounts for Louth Steeple in *Archaeologia*, x. 71: 'riding to the quarrel for stone'. Quarrel is common for quarry. Cf. *New Eng. Dict.*, s.v. quarry.

[20] 'You' interpolated.

[21] 'Have' interpolated.

[22] 'Parte' interpolated.

[Endorsed, fo. 6v] To the right honorable and my owne good Lord, my Lord Henry Clifford, be this deliverd with reverence.

7

John [Wilson] Prior of Mountgrace, to Lord Clifford, 4 *January* [1523].

See introduction, pp. 29, 37. This letter, with its waiting-list of applicants for admission to Mountgrace, claims a place amongst the most important Tudor monastic documents. The year is confirmed by the fact that 4 January in fact fell on a Sunday in 1523. The cousin of Sir William Malleverer about to enter the Carthusian order was Ralph Malleverer, to whose biography our letter makes interesting additions. He was a son of James Malleverer of Seamer, who in 1517 left 'Domino Radulpho, filio meo, j annulum aureum', and other bequests 'Willelmo [i.e. Sir William] fratri meo' (*Test. Ebor.*, v. 83). Ralph became bachelor of canon law at Cambridge in 1518-19 (Venn, *Alumni Cantabrigienses*, s.v. Mauleverer), and soon afterwards, as now shown, commissary and official to John Fisher, Bishop of Rochester. Surrendering this auspicious career, he duly entered the order and ultimately became prior of the Hull Charterhouse. A list of its members in 1536 shows him as prior, then aged 47 (*V.C.H., Yorks.*, iii. 191-2 cites Suppression Papers, ii. 199). In 1535, relates Archbishop Lee, 'the Pryours of Hull and Mountgrace [Malleverer and Wilson] weere sore bent rathre to die, than to yelde to this youre royall style' [of Supreme Head]. Lee then claims credit for winning over both of them: 'the Pryour of Hull, desieringe of me cownsell, I anonne turned from his stiffe opynyon, and made hym yelde with thanks by utterance of the words above written with some oodre' (Ellis, *Original Letters, third series*, ii. 374; *L. & P.*, x. 99). The Hull pension-list (December 1539) is headed by Malleverer, who died on 10 May 1552 (*V.C.H. Yorks.*, iii. 191 gives references).

Mr. William Stapleton was probably the barrister admitted in 1518 to the York guild of Corpus Christi. A younger son of Sir Brian Stapleton of Wighill, he had two brothers in holy orders and a sister Isabel, a nun of Sinningthwaite. He was uncle to the William Stapleton who played a prominent part in the Pilgrimage of Grace, and closely related to Lord Clifford, his mother Joan being a daughter of Sir Lancelot Threlkeld by Margaret, Lady Vescy (J. Foster, *Yorkshire Pedigrees*, ii). 'Burton Abbaye' means Monk Bretton. The name of its subprior at this date is unknown; he is unlikely to have been the Thomas Normanton *alias* Frobisher of 1538, who survived the dissolution by twenty years (J. W. Walker, *Hist. of Monk Bretton* (Y.A.S., 1926) pp. 52, 57). The parson of St. Saviour's, York, probably did not enter the order. Richard Berwick became rector 1513-4, occurs in a will of 1535, and resigned in 1538 (York Diocesan Records, Index of Tudor Clergy, s.v. Berwick; cf. Drake, *Eboracum,* p. 311). On Edward Exley see no. 5 *supra*. 'Mr. Gasquoine' had ostensibly compiled a legal document, and so in all likelihood was Sir William Gascoigne of Gawthorpe, Recorder of York 1523-7; d. 1551 (J. Foster, *Yorkshire Pedigrees*, i; see no. 41 *infra*). At this period knights were frequently styled 'Mr'. The 'ankar' to be licensed by the writer doubtless belonged to the anchorage, the foundation of which Wilson had discussed in no. 6 *supra*. 'Our reverend father' means the Prior of the Grande Chartreuse, who was receiving offerings with a view to the admission of Clifford to confraternity on his death. Thomas Cromwell and Rowland Lee were later admitted to a similar status (D. Knowles, *The Religious Orders*, iii. 234). Dan John Mylde is mentioned by the Carthusian record (cf. *supra*, p. 28, n. 74) as dead in 1518, and he may well have died in the previous year. On the insertion of Clifford's own name in these same records, cf. *supra*, p. 28.

Autograph.

(fo. 7)

Jhesus Maria

Ryght honorable, and my singler good Lord in Our Saveyor, affter my dewte of recommendacion, plesith it your Lordship to understond that I receyved your lettre dated the xiij^th^ day of Decembre, & doith well perceave the contenttes of thsame. And, my Lord, os to your chaplane, I lyk hym well & trustes his calle be of God. Albeit, allthing that apperith good cumyth not onelie of God, wherfor wee in our ordre shuld receyve none[23] withowt perfiett knowlege at thei have long tyme contynued in desire therto. Wherin if they fynd them selffe fyrme & stable, that is a speciall tokyn at they be called of tholie Gost; & for lake of due probacion in the premisses haith grete inconveniences fallen in our religion, os your Lordship knowith; & besides this, our religion is straitt, wherfor it is vere necessarye that he wich thinkith hymsellffe called of God therto shuld exersice hym a yere or two in the straitnes theroff, os in fasting, weering, waking and in solitarie liffing, wich is hard for wordlie men. Moreover, my Lord, wee have bot two celles voide & for thone wee have promysed

[23] 'None' interpolated.

to receyve shortlie affter thfest of thepiphanie a worshipfull man. Sir William Maleverey & he is brether childre, & also he is both commissarie and officialle toth Bushop of Rochester & may spend better then xl[li] beneffesse. His habbett is made redye for hym, and thoder celle is not perfietlie finished. Ther was a monke in it a yere & more, and be cause I thought it[24] nedfull to be mended, putt him in another celle. Albeit, I had promised it to Mr William Stapilton, who I here[25] say is departed fro this wretched liffe, whos soule Jhesus pardone. And affter hym, wee grannted the supprior of Burton Abbaye, and then the parson of Sancte Saveyor in York, and then a yong prest wich was shaven with husse v yere sence, & had such temptacion when he was novace, that he wold nott tare, & soo departed; who had mervelousse grete troble affter, os he saith, bot onely by miracule of Our Blissed Lady he had loost his witte: & thus he is grannted, if he tarre to[26] thos be served wich wee promised be ffore. And yesterday I receyvyd a lettre from a graduett of Cambrige, wich saith he had a grannte in my predecessor tyme, with diversse other that makith grete instance for the same intent. And notwithstanding the premisses, your Lordshipp shall & maye rewlle me & my brether at your plesor. I was mynded to have send my brother proctor[27] to your Lordship shortlie, albeit I trust it shall not nede, for your servand Edward Exley haith promised to cause me have a awnswer, if it be your plesor. Except your Lordship help with your graciouse almose, wee er like to have noo masse, for ther is noo wyne to git in our countre, & that little we have, I fere me, will skarce serve to Eister, wherin I besek your Lordship of succor. Also I am counseld to write the licence for thankar my selffe, of your Lordshipes desire, & so I think it best. I intend to send xl[s] at the leste to our reverend father for your monachate, and shall promisse them your reward when it shall plesse Our Lord take yow to his mercy, wherin I desire your plesor. Dan John Mylde mother recommend hir to your Lordship & thankith the same for your reward, & saith she haith noo succor bot onelie your Lordship. I desire your Lordship to send me the writtyng of Mr. Gasq[uoi]ne with the nextt that comyth, wich Mr Topliffe promised me to doo. And thus, my owne good Lord, thrugh thelp of our Saveyor your Lordship shalbe sure of me to

[24] 'It' interpolated.
[25] 'Here' interpolated.
[26] I.e. until.
[27] I.e. procurator; the monk in a Carthusian house entrusted with the temporal administration and care of the lay brothers.

thottermost of my power, who ever preserve the same with much honor to his plesour. At Mountgrace, this Sonday after matyns, the iiij[th] day of Januarie, with thand of your dailie & nightlie orator,

John, ther prior
Immeritus.

[Endorsed, fo. 7v] To the honorable and his singuler good Lord, my Lord Henry Clifford, at Berden thes be deliverd.

8

John [*Wilson*], *Prior of Mountgrace, to Lord Clifford, fourth Sunday in Lent* [15 March 1523].

See introduction, pp. 35-6. Prior Wilson gives Clifford particulars of a dispute with the Nortons of Bilbrough concerning lands supposedly conveyed to Mountgrace by Robert Norton, brother of Wilson's predecessor. The Priory had been relying upon a collateral warranty executed by Robert Norton, but the judges, to whom the case had been submitted for an opinion, thought this document invalid. The Nortons denied that they had ever discharged their rights by a release, and 'shewid two fare tales' limiting the estate to them and their issue. 'It was not always easy to use collateral warranties, for it needed the co-operation of other members of the family and also depended upon relatives dying in the proper order, conditions which were not always available. When they were, a collateral warranty was a very effective bar to the issue in tail' (T. F. T. Plucknett, *Concise Hist. of the Common Law*, 4th edn., p. 584). It seems nevertheless possible that some of the Norton lands remained in the possession of Mountgrace; the *Valor Eccles*., v. 84 shows the house holding lands and tenements in Bilbrough worth £8 per annum.

The editor knows no satisfactory pedigree of Norton of Bilbrough; for particulars concerning several contemporary members, see *Test. Ebor.*, iv. 92. 'Sir' Robert Norton may have been merely the chantry priest mentioned in the wills of Sir Ranulph Pigot in 1503 and of Jane Stapleton in 1508 (*ibid*., iv. 215, 274). The two distinguished judges mentioned, Sir Anthony Fitzherbert and Sir John Port, naturally figure in *D.N.B.* This passage shows that Port had become a judge *before* 1525 (the date given in *ibid.*) and suggests that both must have spent much time on the northern circuit. Port bought Yorkshire lands in 1526-7 (*Yorkshire Fines*, i, *Y.A.S. Rec. Ser.*, ii, pp. 45, 48) and both judges were active in the north as late as April 1537, sitting on cases arising from the Pilgrimage of Grace (T. A. Beck, *Annales Furnesienses*, pp. 348-9).

Our letter gives further information concerning the Teesdale purchase from Alane Banbrige (see no. 6 *supra*) for Clifford's anchorage. It then graphically describes the difficulty of carting large quantities of stone 'up a grete hille' by means of 'poore mens catell', weak as they are in the winter season. The juxtaposition of these remarks suggests that the anchorage was in fact that of the chapel on the hill above Mountgrace itself. This is said to have been built in 1515, while Richard Methley's *Epistle* (cf. *supra*, p. 35), which must have been written by 1519, was probably directed to the recluse there. Yet there seems nothing improbable in the notion that in 1523 Clifford was completing the foundation of his anchorage with the permanent dwelling-house, which is still extant. About this date the hermit on the Mount was Thomas Parkinson, whose entertaining biography is given in Foxe, *Acts and Monuments*, ed. Cattley, viii. 745-8.

Autograph.

(fo. 8)

Right honorable, and my owne good Lord in Our Saveyor Jhesu, I humbely recommend me unto your Lordship. Pleasith the same to understond that Mr Fegharbard & Mr Portte haith mocioned me enente the [writtynges *cancelled*] travasse concernyng our landes in Westmorland, & required me to wriete to your Lordship[28] in the same. Mr Norton haith put his matter to them & is content to biede ther ende, but I woolde nott agree therto, unto I knew your plesor therin, & so I have promised Mr Fegharbard that he shalhave an awnswer of Wendinsday next in Alverton.[29] Both the juges haith sene our dedes, & they like them nott; for the warand collateralle, wich was our most strengh, thei say it is nothing worgth, for Sir Robert Norton wich made itt was my predecessor brother & came of the Nortons of Bilburgh; & if he had any land it shuld have gone to them & nottother. Also both Mr John Norton & his son[30] denieth ther relesse & saith thei never knewe of itt, & will make itt good before any judge. Therfor the judges thinkith our dedes not sufficient, & if wee agree nott, that it shall make grette troble & cost, & that we shalbe in jeoparde of lesing itt, for Mr Norton haith shewid two fare tales of the same. Wherfor I besech your Lordship of your best counsell agans[t] the day above apointed. Moreover,

[28] 'Lordship' interpolated.
[29] Northallerton.
[30] 'Son' interpolated.

Alane Banbrige & his wiffe[31] haith made a fyne before the judges of his landes in Teisdalle, wich is by yere xxj^{s} vj^{d}, for the wich I have paid xx^{li} xvj^{s} viij^{d}, be side the costes of the fyne. Also I have paid sence I was with your Lordship to the masons & werkmen vj li. I have ij M archleres hewyn, & soo we tare of nothing bot of lime, wheroff I make all the haste that is[32] possible for me, for I can gitt noo cariage for the stone for no money, be cawsse the waye is fulle & upe a grete hille, & poore men[s] catell is so waike, thei dar nott ventor. Albeit, I make the best shifft with our owne that I can, & trustith to have it borne the next weike afftir this, with the grace of God. Also I cawsed Thomas Grice make a draught according to [?the] dede wich your Lordship cawsed make of the M markes, wich ye have given to our poore house. Mr Fegharbard saith it is sufficient & well made, & also the same wich your Lordship caused make, iff it war seigned with selle of your armes. Therfor, if it plesse you to lett me know your plesor therin, I shall cause[33] them be made upe affter your mynd, with thelpe of Our Lord, who have your Lordship & youres in his blissed tuicion. At Mountgrace, the iiijth Sonday of Lentt,

Your owne dayly orator,
John, prior ther.

[Endorsed, fo. 8v] To the right honorable my singler good Lord, my Lord Henry Clifford and Vescy, this be deliverd with reverence.

9

John [Wilson] Prior of Mountgrace, to Henry, Lord Clifford, later first Earl of Cumberland, 27 November [1523].

See introduction, p. 30. Prior Wilson here reports to the heir regarding a further land-purchase to complete the benefactions by the recently deceased Lord Clifford. Wilson has also provided 'a true aged man' to go on pilgrimage for the latter, one of the numerous testimonies to a continuing belief in the efficacity of such observances. The lawyer John

[31] '& his wiffe' interpolated.
[32] 'Is' interpolated.
[33] 'Cause' interpolated.

Belbie was Town Clerk of York in 1511 (*York Civic Records*, iii. 34) and appears, e.g., in Star Chamber cases of the period. He was perhaps a younger son of the manorial family at Killerby in Cayton parish. Cf. *V.C.H., Yorks, North Riding*, ii. 432; *Glover's Visitation*, pp. 189, 574. 'Mr. Fitzherbert' again refers to the judge, Sir Anthony (see *supra*, no. 8); 'John Pullen' to that well-known Yorkshire lawyer, John Pulleyn of Killinghall, Reader of Lincoln's Inn, Town Clerk (1507-10) and Recorder (1534-7) of York, (C. Pullein, *The Pulleyns of Yorkshire*, ch. xv, xvi). Sir Thomas Strangeways of Harlsey and Whorlton Castles served as High Sheriff of Yorkshire in 1520, and died aged about 44 in 1525. His mother was a daughter of the fifth Lord Scrope of Masham and his wife a sister of Thomas Lord Dacre. He was among the most important neighbours of the house, and in May 1540 his son Sir James paid £722 for the actual site of Mountgrace. Cf. J. Foster, *Yorkshire Pedigrees*, iii; *L.* & *P.*, xv. 733 (20). The matter discussed with him by the prior on Clifford's behalf remains unknown.

Autograph.

(*Ibid.*, fo. 9)

Right honorable and my synler good Lord, affter due recommendacion in Our Saveyour Criste, plesith it [your *omitted*] Lordship to understond that I have hard of landes that wilbe sold unto the yerly value of xxv^li^ or xl markes, albeit the purchesse is vere sore, os your Lordship may knowe more largely by John Belbie lettre directed to me, who wrote at the instance of Mr Fizherbertt, os it apperith by both ther lettres herin enclosed. And in case it like your Lordship wee mell herwith, we must pay one hundreth markes in hand & the residew the next tern [*sic*], when the land shalbe made sure. Wheroppon I have sent for John Pullen to be at our house of Sonday or Monday nextt, for to see the evidence & to have his counsell herin. And I desire to know your Lordshippes plesor in the same. Moreover, my Lord, I have spokyn with Sir Thomas Strangwais concernyng the matter your Lordship did commande me, and I cannot perceave that he intendith noo such matteres. Also I have proveded a true aged man to goo pilgrimage for my Lord your father, & have promysed your Lordship will gyve him a gowne, albeit I think best he tarre too the spring of the yere. And thus our mercyfull Saveyor ever preserve your Lordship with mich honor. From Montgrace, the xxvij^th^ day of Novembre.

Your faithfull orator,
John, ther prior unworthe.

[Endorsed, fo. 9v] To the right honorable Lord, my Lord Henry Clifford, this lettre be d[elivere]d.

10

Richard Methley, Monk of Mountgrace, to Lord Clifford, 3 *October* [? *c.* 1510-1515].

On Richard Methley see introduction, pp. 34-5. The year of this letter remains uncertain, but there is no need to assume it very much earlier than the rest of this group. Methley may well have survived throughout most of the second decade of the century and the letter probably belongs to his last years.

'Bill' can mean at this period almost any kind of legal document, sometimes even an inventory or an ordinary letter (cf. *infra*, no. 38, endorsement). In this case it might refer to a deed of gift from Clifford to Mountgrace, the date of which Methley had detached, owing to the delay he mentions, and pending the final approval of its terms.

Autograph.

(fo. 10)

My Lord in Cryste, most singuler beluffyd, after al dew salutacion & hertely thankes for many thynges paste: please it the same to know that I thowgth to have send your Lordshype on byll with a veray treasty man, bot hys mater do brake off, & now I send you the same inclosyde, to looke how you lyek it.[34] Bot the date I cutte of. Fro Mownt Grace, the thirde day of October,

By your beedman
Rychard Metheley,
monke of the same.

[Endorsed, fo. 10v] To my moste worshypefull Lorde, Lord Henry Clyfforde, be this delyverd in haste.

[34] 'It' interpolated.

11

Henry, Abbot of Roche, to the first Earl of Cumberland
[*undated; ? c.* 1535].

See introduction, pp. 37-8. This letter is hard to date with precision. The time of Henry Cundall's election seems unknown, but was probably not long before the dissolution (J. H. Aveling, *Hist. of Roche Abbey*, pp. 71-2). He signed the deed of surrender on 23 June 1538, along with this unsatisfactory monk Thomas Acworth (*ibid.*, pp. 84-6). On the descent of the foundership to the Earl, see *ibid.*, pp. 59, 83. On that of the manor of Maltby to the Cliffords, see J. Hunter, *South Yorkshire*, i. 262; Roche was in the parish of Maltby, and the bailiff would form a natural link between the Earl and the abbot. Thomas Acworth seems to have gone some 20 miles to Tuxford on the Great North Road, to catch the Earl on one of his London journeys. The present letter was written to the Earl on a later visit to London, but since he went so often no certain date can be deduced.

'Our visitor' was some other abbot of the Cistercian order, which had exemption from episcopal visitation. Wolsey had committed all the Cistercian houses to the visitatorial supervision of the Abbot of Waverley, but on his fall they came again under foreign control. To avoid this, a royal commission in April 1532 appointed the Abbots of Fountains, Woburn, Byland, St. Mary Graces and Neath as visitors of the order (*L.* & *P.*, v. 978(6); cf. G. R. Elton, *Star Chamber Stories*, p. 152).

Autograph.

(fo. 11)
Honorable Founder, in my moste lawlest and humeble maner I recommende me unto yow, and even so I thanke your goode Lordeshipe for your grett goodenes done unto me and to your awne perpetuall beidhouse, and also for youre grett and profunde counnsell that your saide hon[our] did giff to my breder at Doncaster. Wherfore we can never be hable to make your saide Lordeshipe condinge recompence bot with oure moste entere daly prayers, which yow shalbe assurede upon, as we ar much bownden so to doo. Ande dowtles, my Lorde, if wee or our monasterye, which is of your noble fundacion, be wrongfully vexed or synistrally entreatted by any of our adversaries, than wee can noo farther bot onely unto youre goodnes for rightwus aide, succ[ou]r and counnsell. And also, my

Lorde, I wolde have written or spoken with yow many tymes or now, both for your helpe and counnsell in many maters, bot that I never dirst be so bolde to call so offte & putt youre saide hon[our] to busynes, or to vex yow. Bot surely, my Lorde, I and my breder may be now more bolde to call of your hon[our] in our neides than we have done[35] yit hyderto. For one writtyng or worde of youre mowth, as we know well, may do more goode to hus than many other in our cunctreth [*sic*] abowt hus, wher of both I and my breder youre faithfull daly orators desyres & praes therof, and to contynew as yow ever have beyn oure goode and graciouse founder, os oure most truste it is.

Also, my Lorde, as I perceiff by youre baillyee of Maltby, youre saide hon[our] haith beyn wrongfully informed that one of oure breder Dan Thomas Acworth shuld faire worse, for because that he cam to youre Lordeshipe at Tuxffurth the last tyme that your hon[our] was at London bott now. Now dowtles, my Lorde, that is nott of a trewth, and that I report me unto hym selff and to all my breder. And as for his office of the priorshipe, dowtles, my Lorde, I putt hym to it to proff hym what he could doo, and in his tyme he did bot veray little, in so much that our order did decay sore under his[36] handes, be cause that he wolde take no payn, bot all outwardes, as he had beyn a temporall man, using ryatt, as schotynges & metynges with any man that wer so disposed. And if that I said any thing to hym therfore, he did allwaiez lightly regarde it, and no menes ther was in hym, for all that I could say. And than shortly affter, oure visitor cam to visitt hus as his dewty was, and than my breder did complean unto hym and tolde hym affter what maner the saide broder did use his office, not affter the forme of relygion; and than both he and all other officers were clerely discharged apon ther offices. And trewly, my Lord, the said broder many tymes & in like caise so did he to our said visitor to be dispensed with of the priorshipe, and putt hym to any other what he wold. And than it was putt to my saide breder by all our consentes to electe all new officers, and than thei putt hym to be the kitchyner, which is a good office if it were well handled, bot it gooith al far in ruyn ande decay under his handes as ever did the priorshipe, and that I report me to all my breder. And if it please your hon[our] to sende privay word emonges

[35] 'Done' interpolated.

[36] 'His' interpolated.

all our breder to know if it be thus or noo, than you shall know more peravent[ure][37] than I [w]ritt, for he[*one or two words obliterated*] that m[a]n yow take hym [*possibly one short word torn away*] if yow knew hym os othe[r] sum doith.[38] And thus Jesu preserve [you]r Lor[deshipe in] bodyly and gostly helth, Amen. Frome Roche, in grett hast the last Sat[urday],[39]

By your daly beideman and
faitfull oritor, Henry, thabbot
of the same place.

[Endorsed, fo. 11v] To the right honorable Lorde Henry, theirle of Comberland, be this d[elivere]d in hast.

12

Richard, Abbot of Shap, to the first Earl of Cumberland,
26 *April* [?1537].

See introduction, p. 31. Richard Bagot was abbot of Shap by 1535 and heads a pension-list dated 13 January 1540 (Dugdale, vi. 870). The Earl was using Bagot to collect arrears of rent from his Westmorland tenants, and since large arrears are most likely to have accumulated during the Pilgrimage, 1537 seems at least a feasible date. On the descent of these manors, see Nicholson and Burn, i. 577 *seqq*. At this period the Cliffords were not using Brough, which in 1521 had been accidentally gutted by fire and was only rebuilt (1661) by Lady Anne Clifford (*infra*, p. 136).

Signed.

(fo. 12)
Pleas it your honorable Lordship to be advertised that wher your saide Lordship dide sende unto me serteyn instruccions concerninge the areragiez of your tenantes of Soureby ande Burghe, ther was iiij poore men of your said tenantes of Soureby twies with me, albeit at the writing heirof ther was no payment maide accordinge to your

[37] 'Peradventure' interpolated.

[38] We should probably read: 'he is not that man yow take hym for, if' etc.

[39] The rest of the line is torn away, but the space available suggests that 'Saturday' was in fact the final word.

Lordshipes pleasor. But I am enformed that they will com yn, ande accordinge to your Lordshipes pleasor use them selfes.
Ande as for your Lordshipes tenantes of Burghe, at the writinge heirof I dide nothinge heir of them.

My moost singuler bowndon goode Lorde, I humblie desier your Lordship to be goode lorde unto Raulf Frear, concerninge his tenement that he holdith of my father Abbot of Beghlande ande his brether, which, by myght of serteyn gentilmen of the contrey, he is like wrongfully to be putt froo (as he saithe) to his utter undoinge, onles that your Lordship wolde of your goodnes take him, his children, his brother ande his saide tenement in governance. Accordinglie (as he shewede me) thate my father abbot of Beghland did instannt[40] your Lordship; by reason wherof he myght enioy his saide tenement in quietnes. Thus the Holie Trinite ever preserve your Lordship in myche honor long to continue. From your poor beidhouse of Shapp, the xxvjth day of Aprill, by your continuall & humble orator,

Ric[hard], thabbot of same.

[Endorsed, fo. 12v] To the righte honorable and his moste singler bowndon goode Lorde and fownder, therle of Comberlande, delyver this.

13

William, Abbot of St. Mary's, York, to the Abbot of Shap, 6 July [1534].

See introduction, pp. 31, 39. Thornton writes the present letter from Overton, the chief country house of the wealthy abbots of St. Mary's; it lay about three miles from York and was rebuilt in 1506 (Dugdale, iii. 540). In Overton also lived the abbot's friend Mrs. Robinson (*supra*, p. 38). The tithe of Bolton refers to Bolton in Westmorland: cf. no. 14 *infra*. This matter relates to the disgrace of the Dacres (*supra*, pp. 23, 48) and the date 1534 is thereby supplied both for this letter and for no. 14. Sir Christopher Dacre was an uncle of William Lord Dacre (Clay, pp. 37-8; *L. & P.*, ii(2). 4541).

Signed.

[40] Urge; cf. *New Eng. Dict.* for several Tudor examples.

(fo. 13)
In my right hartie maner I commend me to you, evenso thankyng the same for your especiall kyndnesse, that it pleased you to move my Lord of Cumberland in my cause & our house. And where ye wryte to me enenst the tyeth of Bolton for my said Lord, trewthe it is, I am not very sure after what maner it was dymyssed to Sir Christopher Dacre. But in case by any meane [?it] retorn to my handes, I shalbe very gladd to grant my said Lord the preferment therof, trustyng therby to opteyn his Lordshippes favores as I have hadde before tyme. And if so happen, then I trust his Lordshipe will consydre partely for his ingresses[41] as other wold do. I wold be very glad of his favores and other suche noble men, as knowyth Our Lord Jhesu, who ever have you in his blessyd tuytion. At Overton, this vj[th] day of July,

Yowr luffer William,
abbot of Yorke.

[Endorsed, fo. 13v] To the right worshupfull and hys syngular freynd, thabbott of Shappe, d[elivere]d.

14

William, Abbot of St. Mary's, York, to the first Earl of Cumberland, 4 September [1534].

See introduction, pp. 31, 39, and no. 13 *supra.* Edmund Whalley, Thornton's predecessor, was confirmed abbot in March 1521 and died in 1530 (Dugdale, iii. 539; *V.C.H., Yorks.*, iii. 111). In December 1534 Cromwell gave Cumberland the ecclesiastical stewardships formerly held by Lord Dacre, so long as Cumberland should be Warden, but he provided that Dacre should continue to receive the fees arising from these offices (*L.* & *P.*, vii. 1549(2)). Cromwell's list does not mention the stewardship of St. Mary's lands in Cumberland, which, granted to the Earl by the present letter, presumably remained with him until the dissolution. The Dacres had other stewardships unmentioned by Cromwell's list; in 1535, for example, Lord Dacre was chief steward of Egglestone and his uncle Sir

[41] I.e. pay ingress-money on being assigned these tithes.

Christopher steward of those lands of Warter Priory which lay in Westmorland (*Valor Eccles.*, v. 126, 237).

Signed.

(fo. 14)

Right honorable, and my full synguler good Lord, in my most humble maner I recommend me unto your good Lordshippe, sygnyfyeng the same I have receyvyd the Kynges most honorable lettres myssyve, dated at Windsore the xviij^th^ day of this last moneth of August, wheryn it is hys gratious pleasor that I shuld grannt unto you the stewerdship of the landes of this monasterie in Comberland, whiche offyce the Lord Dacre lately had; wherwyth I am well contentyd that your Lordship shall entre unto the same office acordyng to the Kynges most dread commandment. And concernyng the teythe of Bolton in Westmorland, the late Abbot Whalley my predecessor, whose soule Jhesu pardone, dyd grannt the same to Sir Christopher Dacre knyght by convent seale for terme of yeres, for the whiche he payd to thuse of thys monasterie a good some of money. And in so myche as the convent seale therof is owt of my handes, I shall shortly wryte to Master Cromwell to shew the Kynges Hyghnes how the same teythe of Bolton standeth. And opon advertisement of hys Graces farther pleasor heryn, I shalbe gladd to do you pleasor with my prayer and service duryng my lyfe, as I and my brether ar bond to pray to Our Lord Jhesu for the preservation of your good[42] Lordship long to endure. At Seynt Mary Abbey nyghe York, this iiij^th^ day of Septembre,

Yowr Lordshippes humble
beedman William, abbot
of the sayme.

[Endorsed, fo. 15v] To the right honorable and hys synguler good Lord, therle of Comberland, d[elivere]d.

(fos. 14v, 15 blank)

42 ' Good ' interpolated.

15

William, Abbot of St. Mary's, York, to the first Earl of Cumberland, 28 October [1530-1538].

See introduction, p. 39. At Kirkby Lonsdale, St. Mary's held the manor, the church, the market and fair, and a jurisdiction of somewhat dubious extent. When in 20 Edward I a *quo warranto* was brought against the then abbot, he claimed assize of bread and beer, a tumbrel and a pillory, but refrained from claiming infangtheof and a gallows. Nevertheless, write Nicholson and Burn (i. 246), 'it seemeth that his successors did not entirely give up all jurisdiction of pleas of the Crown; for the lord of the manor to this day [1777] claimeth and exerciseth a power of appointing a coroner within the said manor.'

Signed.

(fo. 16)

Right honorable, and my synguler good Lord, in my most humble maner I commend me to your good Lordshipe, evenso thankyng the same for your especyall goodnesse towardes me and our monastery, besechyng you of contynuance. And where I am informed that your balyf haith tached one felone withyn our liberties of Kyrkby Lonesdale and impresoned hym in Appleby Castell, this shalbe humbely to desire your sayd Lordshipe to permytt and suffre the goodes and catalles of the same man to remane withyn our sayd libertyes under our balyves custodye, unto suche tyme the Kynges lawes have procedyd upon the same man acordyngly. In doyng wherof, your Lordshipe shall not onely shew your self to be conformable to the Kynges Hyghnes most honorable grauntes, but evenso bynd me and my brethern to pray to Our Lord Jhesu for thenhanncement of the same in myche honor. At Overton, this xxviij[th] day of Octobre,

Youre humble beadman,
William, abbott of York.

[Endorsed, fo. 17v] To the right honorable and my synguler good Lord, therle of Cumberland.

(fos. 16v, 17, blank)

16

William Burbanke to Lord Clifford, 18 *July* [1518].

See introduction, pp. 29, 39. 'Master Herry Martyn', who was acting as agent for Clifford, may well have been the contemporary Henry Marton of Marton in Craven. Cf. the pedigree in *Craven*, at p. 88. The 'right dere servant' of the French King was Nicholas de Neufville, Lord of Villeroy, who on 9 July had signed articles with Henry VIII and Wolsey relating to a marriage between the Princess Mary and the Dauphin, and to the surrender of Tournai (*L.* & *P.*, ii(2). 4303; cf. *ibid.*, 4304, 4339, 4351, etc.). He was to sign the so-called Treaty of Universal Peace on 2 October (*L.* & *P.*, ii(2). 4470, *et seqq.*). Burbanke's forecast of the plans for Campeggio's reception on 23 July compares closely with the actual event described in Brit. Mus. Harleian MS 433, fo. 293 (*L.* & *P.*, ii(2). 4333). 'Lord Burguynye' is one of the many contemporary spellings applied to Lord Abergavenny, who met Campeggio at Dover along with the Bishop of Chichester. At the Blackheath meeting the Bishop of Durham accompanied the Duke of Norfolk and pronounced the welcoming oration; at St. Paul's the Bishops of London and Lincoln were present, but Winchester is not mentioned. On the war between the Turk and Ismael Sophi, King of Persia, the government was well informed. Numerous reports remain in the statepapers for 1517-8 (*L.* & *P.*, ii. *passim*); on the successes of the Sophi, see *ibid.*, ii(1). 2362, 2457.

Readers of this letter should not overlook the last sentence begging timber from Clifford. This reminder was doubtless at the forefront of Burbanke's mind when he troubled to write a rather elaborate epistle to one so remote from the political mainstream as Lord Clifford. Wolsey's request on Burbanke's behalf (no. 20 *infra*) should probably be dated the following November, Clifford having proved dilatory in his response to the present letter.

Autograph. The signature is oddly, but quite clearly, spelt Busbanke, but the hand is certainly that of Burbanke.

(fo. 18)
My Lorde, I commende me hartly unto your goode Lordship. As touching the goode exspede of Master Herry Martyn in your causes, your Lordship shalbe informyde at lengthe by hym. Other newes fewe we have, other then he can shewe unto you. Bitwixt the Kinges Grace and France, we looke to have firme and inviolable peax. A

right dere servant to the saide King of France haith been here of a goode and long season, boith with the Kinges Grace and my Lordes, wher right goode matier and ordynances be comonyde uppon and in maner concludide, for the welth and comforth, peax and amytie of the said realmes, whiche also we trust shall fynally growe to an universall tranquyllitie. A cardinall is comyn from Rome to Calice, wher he haith taryyd a good space [*words obliterated:* ? and shall] shortlie entre into this realme. He bryngith with hym commyssion fro[m t]he Popis Holines for my Lordes Grace and hym self, for to move the Kinges Grace to an universall peax to be astablishide emonges all Christen princes, whiche his Holines haith commandide to be kepide for the terme of v yerres next, under gret peans of cursyng and interdiccion of realmes and landes. He comyth also to desire ayde and support for an enterprise and resistence to be maide aganst the Turke, whoos malice and invasion the Pope gretlie dredith. My Lordis Grace shall now be legatus a latere, that is to have in maner the Popis auctoritie in verray mony thynges. His honor herby shalbe duble asmoche as to be oonlie Cardinall. This forsaid cardinall shalbe honorablelie acceptide. At Dover shal meat hym the Busshop of Chichester and the Lord Burguynye, with other gret company; at Canterbury tharchbusshop of Canterbury in pontificalibus, with certan other busshops and estates. At blake heith shall meate hym my Lord of Northfolke, Duresme and other[43] to the nombre of xv, and knyghtes above xxxij. At Poules Churche my lorde of [Duresme, *cancelled*] Wynchestre in pontificalibus and sundrie other; all thies in their best array and accompany[ed] with gret and riche apparill and gret nombre of people. We looke also to have goode peax with Scotlannde. And so I pray our Lord God to grannt us to have with every Cristian realme. Marvalus soore werr is bitwixt the saide Turke and gret Sophy now [*a word obliterated*] King of Percye, who be boith of right marvalus gret power of people and contries. It is gretlie drede that the Turke is more strong, and yit have we word that the Sophy ferith hym right litle. Our Lorde Jhesu contynue them in contynuall suche amytie, to our rather tranquyllitie. And, my Lorde, with your kynde remembrance of som tymbre, most hartlie fare your good Lordship well. From London, the xiiij[th] day of July.

Your loving chaplan,
William Busbanke, p[rie]st.

[43] I.e. other lords.

[Endorsed, fo. 18v] To my verray singuler goode Lorde, my Lorde Cliffordthe.

17

Brian Higdon, Dean of York, to Lord Clifford, 3 October [1520].

See introduction, pp. 29, 41-2. Londesborough was an important Vescy and Clifford manor; the brass of Lord Clifford's mother remains in the church. In 1535 the clear value of the rectory was £16 (*Valor Eccles.*, v. 141); more than the average for the York diocese. The only vacancy at Londesborough between 1516 (the date of Higdon's appointment) and 1523 (Clifford's death) was in 1520, when the rector Robert Lister died and was succeeded by Anthony Appilby. Cf. York Diocesan Records, Index of Tudor Clergy, s.v. Lister; Appilby. The surname may suggest that the latter derived from the Clifford estates in Westmorland, but does not, of course, prove him to be Clifford's nominee, here refused by Higdon.

Autograph. The hand has some Italianate characteristics.

(fo. 19)

Right honorable, ande my goode Lorde, in my right humble maner I recommende me unto your Lordshippe. Ande where ye dide of lait presente your clerke unto the church of Lonesburgh of your patronege, surely I cane not (of my conscience) admytte hym to itt, fore his connynge is marvyllus slendur. I have seyne few prestis so symple lernede in my liffe. If itt please you to commande some of your lernede chapplens to oppoise hym in your presence, I dowte not butte ye shall perceyve the truth. Ande fore the lakke of his[44] lernynge (which is manifeste) I do putte hym bakke, ande fore noyne oder cause, nor at no mannys desire or motion. Fore of truth I was never desirede by any person to putte hym by. Ande if I hadde be, I wolde not have do itt fore that cause. I truste that I am not so symble, oder to admytte any man or to reiecte any man [any *cancelled*] att the desire of any person, butte accordynge to ther habilities. Notwithstandynge, I do perceive by your Lordeshippe lettre that ye be oder wies informede, butte if itt wolde please you to cause such person as gaffe to you informacion to maike proffe there of, or elles to faill

[44] ' His ' interpolated.

there in, then ye shall know the truth, ande I will thynke me the more bownd to do to your Lordeshippe servyce. And Jhesu preserve your goode Lordeshippe. Frome York, the [iij. *cancelled*] thirde daie of October. By thande of your servande ande beedeman,

Brian Higdon.

[Endorsed, fo. 19v] To the right honorable ande my goode Lorde, my Lorde Clifford.

18

Brian Higdon, Dean of York, to the first Earl of Cumberland, 11 September [? *c.* 1530].

See introduction, pp. 41-2. The Augustinian Priory of Bolton was the chief monastic neighbour of Skipton and Barden; the Shepherd Lord is said to have studied with the canons (cf. *supra*, p. 20). Prior Richard Moone had been elected in 1513 and would be elderly at the date of this letter: the matter he should have been discussing with Higdon was evidently his own resignation. In fact, he continued in office until the surrender in January 1541, and died soon afterwards, his will being proved at York 28 July 1541 (*V.C.H., Yorks.*, iii. 198-9 gives references).

North Ferriby near Hull, a small house of Augustinian canons of the order of the Temple of the Lord at Jerusalem, was in 1526 valued by Higdon himself at £48 clear annual value; in 1535 at £60 (*Valor Eccles.*, v. 129). Its last years saw a quick succession of priors, ostensibly by collusive action in order to secure pensions. On the resignation of Thomas Burgh in June 1532, Brother John Baudewynne, late vicar of Ferriby, succeeded as prior. Burgh then assumed the same vicarage. In September 1534 Baudewynne resigned on a pension and Brother Thomas Androwe was elected. Yet in June 1535 Androwe was pensioned and Baudewynne returned to the priorate, all three being still alive at the dissolution in August 1536 (*V.C.H., Yorks.*, iii. 242). The latest possible date for our letter is thus 11 September 1535, but the last sentences do not seem to have been written during the rapid changes of 1532-5. A date about 1530 is more probable. The Earl's interest in Ferriby is easy to explain, since he was its chief steward, the original founder being his ancestor Henry Bromflete, Lord Vescy (*Valor Eccles.*, v. 129). The Thornton from which Higdon wrote was almost certainly that 4 miles S.W. of Pocklington, which lay in the peculiar of the Dean of York, its patron and appropriator.

Signed.

(fo. 20)

Right honorable, ande my singular goode Lorde, in my moste humble maner I recommende me unto your goode Lordeshippe. Ande opon Saterdaie laste I dide receyve your right honorable lettres (dat the xth daie of Auguste) ande as yit the Prior of Bolton hath not brokyn with me of the mater wherof your Lordeshippe doth write. Ande if he do hereaftur, ande will go forwarde with the same, I shall endev[our] my self in the beste maner I cane to do that thynge which shalbe to the pleasur of Godde for the well ande profett of the house, ande as shalbe also to your pleasur (I truste), for I do perceyve right well that it shalbe necessarie to have ther such a prior as shalbe both wise, ande also quikke ande sharpe, if he shall rewle well that convente. But wher such a man shalbe founde I knaw nott, for I am butt lightly acqwayntide with the brether ther. Ande your Lordeshippe maie be right well assuride that if ye hadde nott written to me in the mater, yit I wolde nott have procedide to any conclusion unlesse I hadde knawne afore both your consaill ande pleasur as anenst the same. Ande as concernynge the house of Fereby, I have nott harde afore butt that it shulde be in good staite, ande the prior ther a full honeste man ande a goode husbande. Albeit, I shall now looke somewhat better unto hym ande to the house both, for the weill of it doth stande much in husbandrie, which (if it be not well lokide unto) maie lightly decaie. Ande thus Jhesu preserve your honorable Lordeshippe. Frome Thornton, the xjth daie of Septembre,

Your humble beedeman,
Brian Higdon.

[Endorsed, fo. 21v] To the right honorable ande my singlar goode Lorde, my Lorde the Earle of Comberlande.

(fos. 20v, 21, blank)

19

Thomas Magnus, Archdeacon of the East Riding, to the first Earl of Cumberland, 24 March [1542].

See introduction, p. 42. Magnus refers to the King's recent visit to York. Henry VIII came only once into the north and was at York 18-26 September 1541: hence our date 1542. On the chronology of the royal visit see J. Hunter in *Memoirs. . . of the County and City of York* (*Archaeological Institute of Great Britain*, 1847) and the present editor in *Eng. Hist. Rev.*, liii. 267-71.
Autograph.

(fo. 22)
Right honorable, and myn oune verey good Lorde, after right due and full humble recommendacon unto youre good Lordeshipp. Pleas it the same to wete that I have bene in truste diverse tymes, sithenne the being here of the Kingges Maiestie, that I shulde have bene in company with youre said Lordship and to have rendred and geven unto youe, my good Lorde, due and condigne thankes for the grete and fatt stagge whiche your good Lordeship gave unto me at that tyme; and thoughe I have not doon my duety in that behalf, as it apperteynned, yet youre good Lordeship shalbe well assured of my harty praier and to have me as your loving preiste and beadman, to be redy to doe unto youe such poore and convenient pleasure as may lye in my litle power, by the grace of God, whoe ever have youe, myn oune good Lorde, in his blessed preservacion and grannte unto youe good and prosperous helth with longe life. At Yorke, the xxiiij[ti] daie of Marche,

Your bounden preiste,
T. Magnus.

[Endorsed, fo. 22v] To [the] right honorable and myn es[pecial] good Lorde, therle of C[umbe]rlandes good Lordeshipp.

20

Cardinal Wolsey to Lord Clifford, 17 November [?1518].

See introduction, pp. 39, 41, and no. 16 *supra*, in which Burbanke himself requests timber from Clifford. The present editor has discovered no proof that Burbanke ever built his projected chapel at Greystoke, where the church was collegiate until the Edwardian dissolutions (*V.C.H., Cumberland*, ii. 204-8). Burbanke may have planned to add a chapel to it; alternatively, he may have sought to build or rebuild an outlying chapel in this large parish, which had four such chapels a little later in the century (Nicholson and Burn, ii. 363, 370, 373-4). Whinfell Forest, in the immediate neighbourhood of Brougham Castle, was famous for its oaks. 'There were here anciently oak trees of prodigious growth, particularly three that were called the Three Brothers; the skeleton of one of which yet remaineth, about 13 yards in circumference, a considerable way from the root' (*ibid*., i. 398). Another request for timber from Whinfell occurs in no. 30 *infra*.

Signed by Wolsey, the body of the letter being in Burbanke's hand.

(fo. 23)
My Lorde, I commend me right hartlie unto you. And for as moche as my chaplan Master Burbanke haith in buylding at Graistoke a certan chapell, wherunto the Popis Holines haithe granntide right grete and honorable indulgences of pardon perpetually to endure, as apperithe in bulles under leade theruppon maide; and wher also he haith greate neide of tymbre for the saide chapell, I shall desire you that of your charitie ye woll grannt unto the performance of the saide chapell foure, fyve or sex ookes of the best and most conveynent for the said warkes, forto be taken within youre parke of Whynfell att the chosyng of his carpenter. Wherby ye shall not oonlie do [a *omitted*] thing right acceptable onto God, but also unto me right singuler pleasor, as knouthe Our Lorde, who preserve you. From London, the xvij^th^ day of Novembre,

T. Car[dina]lis Ebor.

[Endorsed, fo. 23v] To my loving Lorde, my Lorde Clifforthe.

21

Cardinal Wolsey to the first Earl of Cumberland, 20 *March* [?1526].

See introduction, p. 32, and no. 28 *infra*. On 26 March 1526 Sir Christopher Dacre (whose nephew William had just succeeded to the barony) protested to Wolsey that it would be hard for him to occupy the shrievalty of Cumberland, to which he had just been admitted, unless he were protected against the Earl, who had entered upon a great part of the lands belonging to that office and let them to divers tenants (*L.* & *P.*, iv(1). 2052). The present letter seems to be Wolsey's response to this situation; it is dated six days earlier than Sir Christopher's appeal, but there is no difficulty in the supposition that Wolsey had prior information concerning Cumberland's behaviour.

Inglewood Forest then measured about 60 miles in circuit and stretched from Penrith almost to Carlisle. Nicholson and Burn (ii. 396-9) explain the origin of the term Queen's Haims, i.e. demesnes. In 1237 Alexander II of Scotland relinquished his claims in the Border counties in return for a grant from Henry III of 200 librates. In 1251 his son Alexander III married Margaret, daughter of Henry III, who confirmed this grant and gave him 5000 marks for her marriage portion. The lands then received the name Queen's Haims, which they retained on their reversion to the English crown in the fifteenth century. An assize of 6 Edward I shows that they embraced the manors of Penrith, Sowerby, Langwathby, Salkeld, Carleton and Scotby. In November 1525 the Earl had sent a memorandum to Sir Thomas Clifford instructing him to press for various offices and leases, most of them formerly held by Dacre. This paper includes the items: 'To remember about the stewardship of Penrith, called the Queen's Hames. To be steward and master forester of Inglewood forest, and the King's receiver general there, if Dacre has not a long grant' (*L.* & *P.*, iv(1). 1763).

Signed by Wolsey, the body of the letter being in Burbanke's hand.

(fo. 24)

My Lorde, in my right hartie maner I commend me unto youe. And whereas I am enformed that ye nowe of late have dischargied certen fermors owte of their fermeholdes, whiche they had in lease by dymyssion of the late Lorde Dacres within the forest of Inglewod and Quenes Haymes, and occupied untill the departure of the said lorde; bireason wherof they be greatly hyndred and dammaged, without any prouffit or commoditie to arise to youe by that soo doing. It shalbe therfore well doon that for avoiding further inquietation of that countrey, ye not oonly suffre the rest of the tennantes to enyoye their leases, but also restore theim again whiche ye have now put out, untill suche tyme as that mattier shall have been here by the Kinges counsaill farther discussed and debated, and that all thinges therin be considred accordingly: which at your commyng up shall not be fayled to be doon, praying youe therefore in the meane season to followe myne advertisement in the premisses: which shalbe and is to the Kinges singler contentacion and pleasour. And thus fayre ye hartely well. At my place besides Westmestre,[45] the xx^th^day of March,

Your lovyng frende,
T. Car[dina]lis Ebor.

[Endorsed, fo. 24v] To my entierly biloved frende therle of Cumberland.

22

Copy of a Letter, probably from Lord Clifford to Archbishop Savage 11 *September* [1503-1506].

See introduction, pp. 29-30. The form 'Most reverend Fader in God' can scarcely have been addressed to any other than an Archbishop of York, though Wolsey's cardinalate, which involved other forms of address, virtually excludes him from the picture. The writer must have been one of the heads of the Clifford family, since he imprisoned the refractory tenant John Dale in his castle of Skipton. He also holds the lordship of Carlton of the King by a grant under seal, paying the King a certain annual 'duty'. A patent roll shows that on 24 March 1503 the Shepherd Lord had been made keeper of the crown manors of Carlton, Bradley, Utley and Lothersdale in Craven, paying £60 per annum (*Cal. Pat., 1494-1509*, p. 313; cf. *L.* & *P.*, i(1). 218, no. 24). As observed (introduction, p. 26), the first Earl in 1540 purchased these manors, but previously to this date they were held by Sir John Carr, to whom the King granted them in 1512-13 (*Craven*, p. 223). These facts indicate that our writer was the Shepherd Lord, and narrow the period to 1503-13. It can, however, be

[45] I.e. York Place.

narrowed still further. 'Sir Richard Dauson, my prest', who plays a prominent part in the story, was the Richard Dawson instituted vicar of Carlton on 7 April 1503, and who died before 10 August 1509 (*Craven*, p. 226; York Diocesan Records, Index of Tudor Clergy, s.v. Dawson, Ric.).

John Dale was in all probability a gentleman. A contemporary namesake in Carlton, almost certainly to be identified with him, had a daughter Jane who married Christopher Ferrand, heir of a gentle family prominent in Carlton from the fifteenth century to the Restoration (*Glover's Visitation*, p. 517; *Craven*, p. 224). The present editor has no certain dates for John Dale, but since his grandson William Ferrand built Carlton Hall in 1584, he would seem to fit neatly enough into our time-scheme.

It remains to indicate with certainty the recipient of this interesting letter. During almost the whole of the material period 1503-9 the Archbishop was Thomas Savage, who died at Cawood on 2 September 1507. His successor Bainbridge was not translated from Durham until October 1508; he received the temporalities that December, and went off the following year on his ill-fated embassy to Rome. The odds are hence heavily upon Savage. Moreover, there is no matter for surprise in an appeal by a crown tenant to this Archbishop, who had been intimately concerned as a special commissioner with the selection of tenants for the crown lands. Cf. *Materials for Hist. of Henry VII* (*Rolls Ser.*, 1877), i. 298; ii. 215. Our letter is thus tied down to the years 1503-6.

It should in conclusion be remarked that another priest named Richard Dawson is mentioned in a Craven will of 1541 (*Test. Ebor.*, vi. 127) and may be identical with a canon of Shap who appears in a York will of 1531 (*ibid.*, v. 324). Encouraged by this discovery, and feeling that the topic of our letter savoured of the mid-Tudor period,[46] the present editor attempted to elaborate a hypothesis that the letter emanated from the first or the second Earl of Cumberland. Yet on further examination, this theory ran into so many near-impossibilities and improbabilities that it had decisively to be abandoned.

Copy in a sixteenth century hand, unsigned and without address.

(fo. 25)

Most reverend Fader in God, in my most hertly maner I recommend me unto your good Lordship; and haith resayvd one ryght honorable and lovyng letter on your behalfe to me directe, with one bill of complaynt made by John Dayll to your Lordship in your said letter inclosyd. Wherby the said John haith shewed unto your Lordship

[46] On tenants and others imprisoned at Skipton by the first Earl, cf. *supra*, pp. 60, 81 and *Craven*, p. 397.

grett iniures & wronges done to hym by me, Sir Richard Dauson my prest & John Gyllotson my servand. My Lord, I dowt not butt your Lordship knawes I have the lordship of Carleton of the Kynges Grace by his wrytyng under his seall, yeldyng his Grace yerly one certane dewte as is comprised in the same. Wherby also I have autorite to lat & sett, charge and discharge at my plesur all such farmeholdes & farmers as belonges to the said lordship. And upon grete causis yeven unto me & my tenantes theyr by the said John Dayll, I commandytt my servantt John Gyllotson to discharge hym sone after Ester last past, so as he myght have provydit for hym selfe in the spryng of the yere. Howe be it, my Lord, his fraward mynd was such that he wold nawther obeye me ne my commandment yeven by my said servant, but contynued thare dayly trowbling his neghtburs, doyng to theym grett iniures, the which movyd my said servand to set hym in my castell of Skypton, not as he supposys in his bill, but in one fare chambre, wher his frendes had resorte & wer with hym both day & nyght, at libertie all way so to provyde for hym as he nedyd, not famysh but in his awne defaulte. Than the said John & other his frendes instantyd my said prest Sir Richard to labur to me & my councell for hym, and my said prest, movyd with pety, wrote to me & my councell for the said John; the which wrytyng movyd me the rawther to command his delyvere owt of my said castell and under one certane forme, the which he haith not performyd, and as appereth not intendes to do, but farther to inforce hym selfe to my trowble & dayle vexacion, wherwith I cannot be content. Therfore, my Lord, I besech your most honorable Lordship to take with me no displesur, ne with my servandes, for that at is done to the said John, for in good faith his demenor haith bene to my somony fold displesurs & dayly trowble of all the lordship of Carleton; as if it shall please your Lordship herafter at any season to call the mater to farther examynacion, ye shall more surely knawe. My Lord, I can in no wysse suffer the said John longer to tary within the said lordship of Carleton, and without his demenor be better, ne within no place where I have rewell. I shall not hurt hym in body ne goodes, in avodyng of wordly clander [*sic*] & at I more fere the gret danger of God, whom I besech have your Lordship in his blessyd kepyng. At Appilby, the xj day of Septembre.

[No endorsement]
(fo. 25v, blank)

23

Anne Clifton to Sir Henry Clifford, later first Earl of Cumberland, 6 *March* [1518].

See introduction, p. 54. 'My unkyll doctore' was Gamaliel Clifton, D.Can.L., a distinguished Cambridge canonist and one of the learned lawyers summoned to advise Convocation regarding the marriage of Henry VIII and Katherine of Aragon. He was a prebendary of York (1500-41), of Windsor (from 1522), of Hereford (from 1528), and finally Dean of Hereford from 1530 to his death in April 1541 (Venn, *Alumni Cantabrigienses*, s.v.; Cooper, *Athenae Cantabrigienses*, i. 78; *Test. Ebor.*, iv. 65). He was a younger son of the elder Gervase Clifton, and so uncle of Anne's husband Robert. By 'Master Sufyer' the writer probably means one of the surveyors of crown lands (cf. e.g. *L. & P.*, iii(2). 3518); the relevance of such an interview is obvious from the last sentences.

Autograph.

(fo. 26)

Right wyrchypfull brodere, I hartyly recowmawnd me unto yow, besechyng yow to be gud brodere to me, and haffyng gret marvell of yowr unkyndnes, that ye wold not be here yowr selfe at thys tyme, nor nowne for yow, for here hays bene all my husbandes hu[n]kkylles & broders and I hayd nobody to speke in all my cawse bot my selfe. And my husbandes frendes[47] thynkes that my frendes ys unkynd, or elles thay sete lytyll price by me, that thay wold nowne of thame be here at thys tyme; and evere gentylwoman myght hayfe trustyd to helpe of hyre broder.[48] I wout I myght hayfe trustyd to yowre helpe, & I knawe no thyng that ye hayfe downe at London [as yyt *cancelled*] for me in all my matteres as yyt, and that hayfe I grette marvell of, seyng that ye hare[49] daly at London. For thorow trustyng of yowr lab[or]e, I ame lyeke to be pute bothe fro Hodsoke & Clifton, for thorow trustyng opon yow, that ye wold hayffe bene gude broder & frende to me, as yowr promies was. I ned not to hayffe rydyne nor gone to London[50] for no matteres, as bot thynkyng

[47] 'Frendes' interpolated.

[48] 'Broder' interpolated.

[49] Are.

[50] 'To London' interpolated.

that ye wolde hayfe spokyn the beste ther for, in my matteres as well as for yowr awn, and that ye wolde hayfe mayd a supplicacion and hayfe put yt upe to my Lord Cardinall in my name; and that hayd bene beste for me, in my mynd. And I wout, ye wolde hayfe spokyn to Master Sufyer and tyll[51] hayffe bene gud frende for me, and to hayffe spokyn to my Lorde Cardinall for me; and yf ye hayd done so, I wold hayff trustyd to hayffe hayd a answere or now. And Sir, ye knawe that yt ys halfe a yere sene my husband departyd, wo Jhesu pardon,[52] and as yyt hays knaw[53] nown answere; and her I ly & kepys hows to my grete coste & charge; and my unkyll doctore schowys me I must pay for al manere of thyng that I hayfe takyng sene my husband departyd. And that [I] ame not abyll for to do, for ye knaw howe I was lefte in grete trobyll & besenes, & lytyll to helpe my selfe with all. Therfor, Sir, I wout that ye wold hayffe spede my matteres mor schortly, that I myght hayffe hayd sume thynge to hayffe trustyd to. And, Sir, bot yf ye wyll be gud brodere to me & speke for me better then ye hayffe don yyt, I knaw no frenchype nor no frende to truste to, bot for to cowme upe my selfe the nexte terme, & labor for my selfe the beste that I cane. And yet[54] ame I lytyll beholdyn to yow & to my syster, and[55] I cane hayff no beter favore at yowr handes bot to labor for my selffe, and therfor, Sir, beseche yow to send me word[56] by the berer her of qwat ye cane do for me in al my matters. And, Sir, I pray you that ye & my broder[57] & my syster wyll speke to gyder & take yowr beste counsell & [ad]vyce qwat ye cane do for me. Also, ye hayffe letyn Clefton be laboryd furthe of my handes, for I knaw hyme that hais a grawnt of hyt; therfor I thynke gret unkynnes in yow, that ye hayffe letyn [? it *omitted*] ben laboryd for me [*sic*]. No mor at thys tyme, bot Jhesu preserve yow. Wrytyn the sexte day[58] of Marche,

By yowr loffyng syster,
Anne Clifton.

[Endorsed, fo. 26v] To my ryght wrychypfull brodd[er] Sir Harry Clyfforthe be thy [*sic*] byll byll [*sic*] deliveryd in haste.

[51] To.
[52] These three words are interpolated.
[53] Known; this word is interpolated.
[54] 'Yet' interpolated.
[55] An, i.e. if.
[56] These four words interpolated.
[57] 'Syster will' is also erroneously interpolated after 'broder'.
[58] 'Day' interpolated.

24

Lady Anne Conyers to the first Earl of Cumberland, 16 *June* [1538].

See introduction, p. 53, and no. 25 *infra*.
Signed. Signet en placard.

(fo. 27)
This bill, maid this xvjth day of June in the xxx yere of the reign of our Souverain Lord King Henry the eght, witnessith me Anne Conyers wedow, Lady Conyers, and one of the exec[utors] of my Lorde my husband Cristofer late Lord Conyers decessid, to have had and receyved by the thandes of my servant William Perkynson of the right honorable and my singuler good Lorde, my Lord Henry Erle of Cumberland, afore hand or afore it aught to be paied by covenant of indentors of mariag of my son John and my Lady his wiff, the summe of one hundreth markes, in parte of payment of the summe of two hundreth markes, payable afor the feast of Sanct Mychell the Archangell[59] next comyng, as by the said covenantes at larg it doth appere; of whiche summe of one hundreth markes I knowleg my self trewly content and payed, and the said right honorable my veray good Lorde his heires and exec[utors] therof fully accquyte and discharged. In witness wherof I the said Lady Anne Conyers wedow, and one of the exec[utors] of my said Lord last will, have her unto sett my seall and subscribed my name, the day and yere abovesaid.
Anne Conyers.

[Endorsed, fo. 28v, in an eighteenth-century hand] Release from the Lady Ann Coniers to the E. of Cumber[lan]d, ann. 30 H[enry] 8.

(fos. 27v, 28 blank)

[59] 29 September.

25

Lady Anne Conyers to the first Earl of Cumberland
[*4 April* 1539 *or* 26 *March* 1540].

See Introduction, p. 53, and no. 24 *supra*.
Signed.

(fo. 29)
Right honorable, and my veray singler good Lorde, with my right hartie comendacions unto the same. Theys shalbe to advertise your Lordshipe that my Lorde my sone and I have bene with my Lorde Privayseall, whose Lordshipe haithe very gentely accepted my sayd sonne, saynge that he wyll putt hyme unto the Kinges Grace service. And forther, my veray gud Lorde, I right hartly desire the same that yt wold plesse your Lordshipe that my Lady your doughter and myne may tary withe your Lordshipe, and at suche tyme as your Lordship dothe come to London ther shalbe found suche a means ther in as shall stand with your own contentacion. And thus the Holie Trynite long preserve your Lordshipe in helth, withe increse of honor, according to your hartes desyre. Frome London, the present Goodfrydaye,

Your Lordshipe own assuredly,
Anne Conyers.

[Endorsed, fo. 29v] To the right honorabyll and my singler good Lord, my Lorde off Cumerlande gud Lordshipe.

26

Thomas, second Lord Dacre of Gilsland, to Lord Clifford,
6 *January* [?1514].

See introduction, p. 30. Disputes were common between the great Border-families over the service-obligations of their tenants. The present one should probably be laid alongside Lord Dacre's complaint in his remarkable letter of 13 November 1513 directed to the King. After his detailed and graphic description of a foray into Scotland, he adds, 'Also pleas it your Grace, me seamnes it were necessary that your lettres of commaundement were direct to my Lord of Northumbreland and to my Lord of Clifford to cause their tenaunts gif attendance opon your Wardens as thei have bene accustomed to do in tymes passed, for as I understond my Lord Cliffords tenaunts er warned not to ride without his speciall commaundment' (Ellis, *Original Letters, first ser.*, i. 97).

The Thomas Wharton here mentioned was the father of the famous first Lord Wharton: he is mentioned in 1512 in an account of Edward Bensted, late treasurer of the wars in the King's army in the north: 'a coat of white and green for Thomas Warton, clerk of the wars, 4s.; his wages at 2s. a day for forty days' (*L.* & *P.*, i(1). 1450). Henry Salkeld was probably a younger son of the well-known family of Corby, Cumberland, and Thrimby, Westmorland (*Pedigrees . . . of Cumberland and Westmorland*, ed. J. Foster, p. 112). He appears as a J.P. making an enquiry at Appleby in March 1515 (*L.* & *P.*, ii(1). 236). Dacre addresses Clifford as 'cousin' and stresses the 'nighenesse of blode' between them. His aunt Joan Dacre had married Thomas, eighth Lord Clifford, the Shepherd Lord's grandfather (Clay, pp. 24, 37).

Signed.

(fo. 30)

My Lord and cousin, I comande me to you, ascertanyng you that has I was ryding thorowe Westmorlande upon Tewsday last passed, it was reaported to me by dyverse and syndry gentilmen, inhabitantes within the countie of the same, that ye of late sent your officers and servantes to Appulby, that is to sey, Thomas Wharton and Henry Salkeld, who in your name and be your commandment sent for all and every gentilman within the same shyre, shewing unto them that I had made complainte to the Kinges Grace and his counsaill of your Lordship and them, for non doyng of your and there dueties to the Wardain of the Marchies in tyme of nede, when as they were wairned. Wherupon your said officers and servantes charged them to certifie you what service or dieutie ye and they oweth, or in tymes passed was accustumed to doo to the Wardain in tyme of werre, when as they were laufully wairned and required, commanding them in generall that they should saye and shewe that they were not wonnt in tymes passed to doo service, nor in tyme comyng shuld serve the King or his Wardain in his absence out of this the Kinge's realme without wages.

My Lord, seyng the nighenesse of blode that ye and I be of (as nature requireth) right sory I am to here any thing sounding to youre dishonestie that mought by neccligency turn to your displeasure herafter, be reason of oversight, beyng soo light of demeanor and wordes as to maike any suche mysreaporte on me to the gentilmen of the countrey, where thorowe the Kinges Highnes should be worse served, both in this his realme and Scotland, herafter aswell in tyme of werre as peas. And over that, sory am I that ye shuld take upon you to use any thing belonging myn office of wardenry without auctorite.

Cousin, I ascertaigne you that I maide noo siche complainte as ye and your servantes has made relacion. Trouthe it is, that I advertised the Kinges most honorable counsaill of late that your tenantes and servantes woold not com to me to doo the Kinges Grace service siche tymes as I invaded Scotland, to the noysannce of the Scottes, when as they were laufully wairned. Wherupon it pleased the Kinges Highnes to write unto you (fo. 30v) his most honorable lettres, commanding you by the same that ye and they at all tymes here after shuld be redy, upon reasonable warnyng by me and my deputies yevin, to serve his Grace and attend upon me his said Wardain for the tyme, according to the auncient custume in our antecessors daies used, which was alwey aswell within Scotland as upon these bordours within this his realme, on there owne charges without wages.

My Lord, hiddertowardes I have not bene oportune in calling upon your servantes and tenantes to doo service like as I haif done to oder of the Kinges subgettes, but has bene favorable to them for youre sake. Wherfor, my Lord, seyng your mysreaporte afore specified, without that ye in haisty wyse woll assemble the same gentilmen to gidders and declare unto them that I made noo siche complainte of you and them as is surmysed, and over that, that they to gidders with your tenantes wolbe attendant at tymes behovefull and necessary, upon wairnyng to be yeven by me or myn officers, to serve the Kinges Grace and me his Wardain now in the tyme of werre, aswell to maike invasions in Scotland from tyme to tyme as the case shall require, according as hath bene accustumed (as to resist the Scottes yf they fortune to entre within these Marchies), I woll shewe and advertise the Kinges Grace and his counsaill of your and there dealinges herin, to thentent that ye and they maye be afore them, and then furthir direction to be takyn by his most noble Highnesse and them, as they shall thinke by there sapience and wysdomes. For as for me, I demande and charge your tenantes and other of the Kinges subgittes non oder wyse but as any oder person beyng Wardain wold charge me and my tenantes in tyme of nede; and as ye wooll doo in the premisses, that I may know your mynde and aunswere at length in writing with this berer. And thus fare your cousinage aswell as I wold my self. At Karlisle, the vj daye of January,

Your lofyng cosyn,
Thomas Dacre.

[Endorsed, fo. 31v] To [?my] Lord and cousin, my Lord [Clif]ford in haist be this delivered.

27

William, third Lord Dacre of Gilsland, to Sir William Parr,
30 *November* [1525].

See introduction, p. 48. On 18 June 1525 young Henry Fitzroy, Duke of Richmond, who was being placed as titular head of the King's Council in the North, received the custody of the city and castle of Carlisle (*L. & P.*, iv(1). 1431(6)). Thomas, second Lord Dacre, died on 24 October after a fall from his horse. He was succeeded as Warden of the West March by the Earl of Cumberland. By this present letter from London, the third Lord Dacre orders his cousin Sir William Parr, chamberlain to the young Duke, to deliver the city and castle to the Bishop of Carlisle (John Kite, 1521-37), for the use of the new Warden. On Parr's inefficiency as chamberlain, see Reid, p. 105. Dacre's grandfather had married Maud Parr, aunt of Sir William. The latter was uncle of Queen Katherine Parr, obtained a peerage in 1543 and died in 1546 (Clay, pp. 157-8). For another aspect of the relations between the Dacres and the Parrs cf. *supra*, p. 50, n. 159.
Signed.

(fos. 30v, 31, blank)
(fo. 32)
Cousin, in my mooste hartie wise I recommende me unto youe, certefieng the same that I am commaunded by my Lorde Cardinallis

Grace to delyver the citie and castell of Carlisle unto my Lorde of Carlisle, who haith auctoritie by commission to receive the same to thuse of my Lorde of Cumberlannde. And further his Grace commanded me to advertise youe therof, to thintent that ye might shew it to all my Lorde of Richemountes counsaill. And forasmiche as I have sent downe at this tyme to my counsaill for the delyvery of the same citie and castell, I do send to youe this advertisement according as I was commannded to do. And thus mooste hartely fare youe as well as my self. Frome London, the laste day of November,

Your lowyng cosyng,
William Dacre.

[Endorsed, fo. 32v] To my cousin Sir William Parre knight, chamberlayn to my Lorde of Richemount Grace.

28

William, third Lord Dacre of Gilsland, to the first Earl of Cumberland, 16 *March* [1535].

See introduction, pp. 48-9, and no. 21 *supra*. Dacre here asks for money due after the reckoning made between them by the King's Council at York. This must be the award in the statepapers corrected by Cromwell towards the end of 1534 (*L.* & *P.*, vii. 1549). Under this, Cumberland had to pay various tithes, rents and fees due to the Dacres, as well as compensate them for corn and other goods seized by Cumberland at the time of Lord Dacre's arrest (*ibid.*, 1549(2), items 3-8). The Lord President mentioned by Dacre was Bishop Tunstall. When in January 1533 the Earl of Northumberland was made King's Lieutenant, he did not displace Tunstall, who continued to hold the office of President and to transact judicial business. Cf. C. Sturge, *Cuthbert Tunstall*, p. 149.

Dacre writes from the castle at Hinderskelfe, which occupied the site of the present formal garden at Castle Howard. Leland (*Itineraries*, ed. L. Toulmin Smith, i. 65) describes it as 'a fair quadrant of stone having 4 toures buildid castelle like, but it is no ample thing'. It was a Greystoke castle, which passed *c.* 1507 to the Dacres, and in 1577 to the Howards, being burned down early in the eighteenth century (*V.C.H., Yorks., North Riding*, ii. 107-110).

Signed. Signet en placard.

(fo. 33)
My Lorde, in my right hertie maner I commande me unto youre good Lordshippe. And where as my Lorde President, the iustices of assise and other of the Kinges mooste honorable counsaill at Yorke hath takin paine in makin of a raykenyng and ordre betwix youre Lordshippe, myne uncle Sir Christofer Dacre and me, as my Lorde youre sonne and other of youre counsaill canne shew youe, desiring youre Lordshippe that my servant this berer may recevey the money of youre Lordshippe according to the said ordre, who I have commandit to deliver unto youe upon the receypte therof acquitans for the same. At this tyme I myster money and muste goy to London, as knowith the Holy Trinite, who have your Lordshippe in his blissed keping. At Hildreskelfe the xvj day of Marcij,

Your Lordshype,
William Dacre.

[Endorsed, fo. 33v] To my Lorde of Cumberland his good Lordshippe.

29

Thomas Jolye, Vicar of Skipton, to the second Earl of Cumberland, 7 January 1549.

See introduction, pp. 33-4. Most of the numerous persons mentioned in the present letter can easily be identified. Thomas 'Jollie' occurs in 1548-9 as vicar of Skipton in the foundation-deed of the school. The list of vicars in Whitaker, *Craven* p. 424 appears incomplete, and does not indicate Jolye's terminal dates; I have failed to locate him in the York Diocesan Records. For Thomas, first Lord Wharton (1495-1568), victor of Solway Moss and most famous Border-commander of his day, see *D.N.B.*; Joan Evans in *Archaeological Journal*, cii. 134 *seqq; Hist. Monuments Comm., Westmorland*, p. 142; plates 122, 123. Sir Richard Musgrave of Edenhall was Wharton's son-in-law, having married his younger daughter Anne or Agnes (*Pedigrees . . . of Cumberland and Westmorland*, ed. J. Foster, p. 93). Nicholas Fairfax was elected M.P. for Scarborough in 1541, and for Yorkshire in 1547 and 1563; for his life see *Parliamentary Representation of the County of York*, ii (*Y.A.S. Rec. Ser.*, xcvi), pp.

5-8. Sir William Babthorpe was a Councillor in the North 1525-55, and M.P. for Yorkshire in 1547 and 1554 (*ibid*., pp. 8-11).

Of the list of M.P.'s engaged by Jolye to speak in the debate, the best known are Sir Robert Broke, Richard Goodrich, Sir James Dyer and Thomas Carus, whose careers are all outlined in *D.N.B.* 'Sampoll' and 'Sampoole' are spellings of St. Paul (E.g. in *Test. Ebor.*, v *passim* and *Y.A.S. Rec. Ser.*, xlv. 50); this old family was of Campsall in South Yorkshire, and Snarford, Lincolnshire; the reference may be to John St. Paul of the former, who died in 1550 (J. Hunter, *South Yorkshire*, ii. 464; *Glover's Visitation*, p. 307; J. F. Horne in *Y.A.J.*, xx. 284-90). 'Lord Governor' reflects Somerset's official title, *personae regiae gubernator ac regnorum dominiorum et subditorum nostrorum protector*. Wriothesley twice calls him 'Lord Protector and Governor'. 'The Lord Grey' was Lord John Grey, prominent later in the year for his part in the suppression of the Western Rising (*D.N.B.*). On the trial and execution of Sir William Sherrington for counterfeiting, see Wriothesley, *op. cit.*, ii (*Camden Soc., new ser.*, xx), p. 7. 'Mr. Eynns' was Thomas Eynns, secretary to Edward VI before his accession, and in 1550 appointed secretary for life to the Council in the North (*Cal. Pat., Edw. VI*, i. 55; iii. 294; cf. Reid, pp. 170, 188, 257). His dangerous association with Sherrington now gives us the answer to the problem posed (p. 170) by Dr. Reid. William Tankard was Recorder of York 1537-73, M.P. for Boroughbridge in 1553 and a Councillor in the North 1566-72 (*York Civic Records*, iv-vii *passim*; G. R. Park, *Parliamentary Representation of Yorkshire*, p. 229; *Glover's Visitation*, p. 216; Reid, p. 494). The Duke of Suffolk whose debts were to be settled was Charles Brandon, who had died 24 August 1545. His son the young Duke, then aged only thirteen, was being educated with Edward VI: it seems hence natural that Somerset should announce the payment of the father's debts. A survey of 1573 shows Clifford's Inn as still being rented (for £4 per annum) from the third Earl of Cumberland (R. T. Spence, *op. cit.*, p. 383).

Autograph.

(for 34)

Pleaseth it your honorable Lordship to be advertised that, being in redines to repayr home upon Saturday last, was put into the Parliament house a byll by Richard Musgrave, which could not be otherwise then by the procurement of the Lord Wharton, & having sent breve lettres theof in post, which I suspect the delyvery, the[se] shalbe to advertise your Lordship that the tenor & effect of the same bill is to take away your inherytannce the Shirifwik of Westmorland; the copy of which bill your Lordship shall receyve by the next post, for that as I cannot have theym tyll to morow, albeit I doubt not but the same shall not procede. Mr Fairfax, Mr Babthorp with so many your Lordshipes frendes hath & will speke in the same, that your counsaill learned doth in no wise fere the matier, & thinketh that it will be no further spoken of; but in case it be redde agayn, I have assurede to speke in it Mr Roper, Mr Gosnall, Mr Sampoll, Mr Brok of London, Mr Goodrych, Mr Dyer, Mr Caruse, lerned in the law, & I trust to have almost the hole house of that parte; & if nede be, my Lord Protectors Grace will wryt to stay, or els send, by occasion wherof the old matier agaynst the Lord Wharton shalbe instantly callede upon, as the Lord Governor hath promysed, and your Lordshipes lerned counsaill will that the bill devysed at your L[ordshipes] last being in the town shalbe exhibit into the Sterre Chamber, & commandment for the Lord Wharton and Richard Musgrave with such other as be in the towne (fo. 34v) to make aunswer the begynnyng of this term. In theise and others your L[ordshipes] affayres I shall so do as in me lyeth, trusting, in case I canne see this act put in by Musgrave discharged, to be at home shortlye. The Lord Dacre hath promysed to joyn with your Lordship agaynst the Lord Wharton, if he kepe promyse, as I doubt not he will. And for ony act or statute past of effect ther is none worthy ony wryting. Ther is oon for making of malte, being the fyrst of this session;[60] a nother for p[rie]stes to have wyves & theym that have wyves to be p[rie]stes & take promocion spirituall;[61] oon moved for alteracion of almost all lawes;[62] oon for fynes to be levyede within the Countie Palatyne of Chester;[63] a book for dayly service in the churche;[64] a like to have a subsidie upon wordes spoken; the Lord Grey as semeth not veray well taken withall; Master Sherington, M[aste]r of the Mynte of Bristow, in ward with Mr Eynns, & a great liklyhod that many of the same facultie shall come to like passe (his goodes seased & servanntes put at liberte). Mr Tankerde cann informe your L[ordshipe] concernyng Clyffordes Inne. I have sent with this berer a testament of herysye, the confession of the maker therof. Her be many leude bookes made dayly & much disputacion for the sacrament of thaulter, albeit in most churches of London dayly dyvers masses seyde, as I have before

[60] 2 & 3 Edw. VI cap.10.

[61] 2 & 3 Edw. VI cap.21.

[62] This curious phrase does not relate to any known bill or statute; just conceivably, it may be a confused impression of the title of 2 & 3 Edw. VI cap.21: 'An Act to take away all positive Laws made against Marriage of Priests.'

[63] 2 & 3 Edw. VI cap.28.

[64] 2 & 3 Edw. VI cap.1.

wryten. (fo. 35) The Lord Governor hath promysed payment of the Duke of Suffolk debtes this terme. And thus, not doubting but your Lordship have good sped in all your affayres, I shall pray for thincrease of your helth & honor. At London, this vij[th] of January 1548,

Your humble orator & servant,
Thomas Jolye.

[Endorsed, fo. 35v] To the right honourable therle of Cumbrelande.

30

Henry Algernon, fifth Earl of Northumberland, to the first Earl of Cumberland, 19 April [1526 *or* 1527].

See introduction, p. 46. The 'Magnificent' Earl wrote this letter to his son-in-law after the latter's elevation to the Earldom in June 1525. April 1526 is a somewhat more likely date than April 1527, since the writer died on 19 May 1527. On the famous oaks in Whinfell Park, see no. 20 *supra*. The Percies were lords of the honor of Cockermouth and probably kept the castle in repair at least until Elizabethan times. Readers of the *Percy Household Book* will recall that the fifth earl resided chiefly at his two East Riding castles, Leconfield and Wressle, at which latter the present message was written.

Signed.

(fo. 36)
Myne nowne good Lord and sonne, in my full hertie manner I recommende me unto youe, my good Lord. I must be asuitor unto youe for somme tymber treis within your Lordship off Wynfild for the maiking up agayne the rouf of my hall within my castell of Cokwmouith, which I canne gett no tymber in that countrie ellis which woll serve me yt. My Lord, I woll gif youe as large for theim as anny man shall. I doo write unto your Lordship for no nomber, bicaus I know not my self as yet, what tymber it woll taike. For when I have knowledge, I woll bebould then to write unto your good Lordship for what I nedde for that caus. And of your goode Lord-

shipis mynde herin I may be advertissid. Writyn at my castell of Wresill, the xix[th] day of Aprell,

Yours assured,
H. Northumberland.

[Endorsed, fo. 36v] To my nowne good Lord and sonnenlaw, my Lord therle of Commbreland.

31

Henry Percy, later sixth Earl of Northumberland, to the first Earl of Cumberland, 16 October [1526].

See introduction, pp. 46-7. Regarding the Norfolk-Wolsey feud, by the following 18 May Mendoza was writing that Warham, Norfolk and Tunstall sought Wolsey's complete ruin (A. F. Pollard, *Wolsey*, p. 221). In view of his cordial letter to his son-in-law (no. 30 *supra*), it seems remarkable that the fifth Earl now urged Wolsey not to trust Cumberland, as being 'all with my Lord off Norffolk'. His charge may nevertheless have been true, since Cumberland had been in trouble with Wolsey earlier in life (*supra*, p. 22). The younger Percy's warm regard for Cumberland, shown by his secret warning in this letter, is borne out by nos. 32-34 *infra*.

The news-items in the concluding passages supply the date. Louis II of Hungary was defeated and killed by the Turks at Mohacs on 29 August 1526; it is somewhat surprising to find this event regarded as 'news', even in England, so late as 16 October. The attack on Rome by the Colonna faction occured on 19 September 1526. The great Sack of Rome was not to occur until the following 6 May; hence this earlier rifling of the papal palace, the cardinals' houses and St. Peter's, still possessed a sensational interest. For letters to England from Rome describing the affair, see J. S. Brewer, *The Reign of Henry VIII*, ii. 95-7. The rumour concerning a Parliament the next Candlemas, i.e. 2 February, was not justified by the event, since no new session actually occurred until the beginning of the Reformation Parliament in November 1529. Percy's reprehensible omission to describe the 'marvelous high cheer' enjoyed by the King on his recent visit to the Cardinal is partially repaired by Spinelli (cf. Brewer, *op. cit.*, ii. 106-8) and by Cavendish (*Early Eng. Text Soc.*, ccxliii. 25 *seqq*).

'My brother Daycar' was William, third Lord Dacre, who like Percy had married a daughter of the fourth Earl of Shrewsbury. 'Pastes of a redere' means pasties of a red deer. 'At nopont' means 'at no point', i.e. not agreed, settled. This cryptic phrase may refer to the disagreements between father and son, or, e.g., to legal business concerning their debts: one is reminded of Heywood's phrase, 'Is he at a poynte with his creditors?' Cf. *New Eng. Dict.*, s.v. point. 'Master Chamberlane' could scarcely apply to the Lord Chamberlain, then Lord Sandes, yet the latter's intimacy with Wolsey in this very year is stressed by Cavendish (*op. cit.*, pp. 26-7). The Great Chamberlain was also a peer: the Earl of Oxford. But this reference may simply be to the chamberlain of Wolsey's own household (he had a high chamberlain and a vice-chamberlain; *ibid.*, p. 20) or to a chamberlain of the Exchequer, or even to Sir Edward Chamberlayn!

Mr. and Mrs. Hercy were perhaps members of the family at Grove, Notts. (cf. *Glover's Visitation*, p. 41). 'The Castell Angell' means the Castello St. Angelo, connected with the Vatican by a fortified causeway allowing safe escape for hard-pressed pontiffs.

Autograph.

(fo. 37)

My weray good Lord, in my most harte maner I recommend me unto your good Lordshipe, ryght interly thankyng the same not onlye for your lovyng letters but also for your kynd rememberance off me with your fatt pastes off a redere, the whych, my good Lord, dyd me, I promes yow, synguler pleasur. And for them the whych ye send unto my Lordes Grace, I promes yow ys Grace dyd tayke them weray thankffully, not withstandyng my brother Daycar had not long be foyr presentyd ys Grace with vj pastes off astag, but the exceptyng off the precens wher not lyke, for I promys yow ys Grace dyd accept yours wery thankfully, for the[65] com unto hys Grace now agenst the Kinges comyng to York Plas. And consernyng my Lord my fayther and me, we be, nor shall not be, at nopont to Candelmes terme, but he showyd my Lordes Grace that ther was no trust in yow, and desyeryd hys Grace to put no conffydens in yow, for ye wer all with my Lord off Norffolk. And thys he sayd oppynly to my Lord, I standyng bye, with many mor wordes than I can wrytt; wer for, my good Lord and brother, I pray yow kepe thys secret and be wery wayre off your selff, for and[66] my Lord my fayther mene do ye ony harme, ye shall be assurydly off yt.

(fo. 37v) My good Lord, for your x^th^ [*sic*] pastes that yow send to

[65] They.

[66] I.e. an, if: the word is interpolated.

my Lord my fayther, I toke apon me to order theme, synce he was gone. Wher ye send my Lord Grace x, I pott ij off thoes yow send my Lord my fayther, and so my Lordes had xijth [*sic*]; ij I gayff M[as]ter Cha[m]b[e]rlane from yow, wo ys wery gret with my Lord; ij I gayff Mres Hercy from yow; and ij to Mr Hercy from yow, wo tok them wery thankffully. And the other ij, my Lord, I was so bold apon yow that I gayff them the Popes embassitor, and thows,[67] my Lord, I deley[?vere]d your x pastes.

And for our occurantes her, the Gret Tork hayth whon all Hungery and slane the Kyng. On off[68] the Emperores cappetayns with the Cardenall off Colunna came in to Rome apon anyght with vij M. horsmen and be segytt the Pop[e] in ys palles, but the Pop[e] fled howth a conceled way and went to the Castell Angell, and so the Neapolletans dyd spowll ys pallas, and had all the rychys that [?he] had: plat, monay and other. But now the Emperor hayth sent unto the Kyng that he wyll byd ys award in all thynges, by reson weroff we trust to have pes in all Crystyndom.

(fo. 38) Also the Kyng was her with my Lordes Grace wher he had marwelus hy sher. And so yt ys sayd ther shall be aparlement at Candelmas next. And thus Our Lord preserve your[69] good Lordship. Wrytyn at London, the xvjth day off Octobur with the rude[70] hand off

Yours assurydly,
Henry Percy.

[Endorsed, fo. 38v] To my weray good Lord brother in law, Lord off Comberland.

32

Henry, sixth Earl of Northumberland, to the first Earl of Cumberland, 28 January [1528].

See introduction, p. 47. There are two clues to the date, neither absolutely certain in itself, yet both pointing to the year 1528. Northumberland notes

[67] Thus.
[68] These two words interpolated.
[69] 'Your' repeated.
[70] This word is almost illegible; likewise its counterparts at the end of letters 33 and 34 *infra*, but this seems the correct reading. Compare 'the rude and raggyd hand' in another letter of the sixth Earl in Fonblanque, *Annals of the House of Percy*, i. 432.

'howe prousperously the Kynges affaires goeth forward here'. Elsewhere he reports from Alnwick his successes in capturing and executing important bands of outlaws on 28 January 1528 (*L. & P.*, iv(2). 3849, 3850). The day and place of our present letter correspond. Again, Morpeth Castle was a Dacre seat, and the Percies had no house there at which they would have met for Shrovetide festivities. Why should Northumberland meet the Cliffords, who were normally antagonistic to the Dacres, at Morpeth? The answer seems to lie in the fact that Northumberland was engaged at the beginning of 1528 in framing an award between his contending brothers-in-law, Dacre and Cumberland; he actually drafted it in his own hand on 26 February 1528 (*ibid.*, 3971). And Shrovetide, when the house-party mentioned in our letter was due to gather, fell in 1528 at the 'right' date: 21-25 February.

Signed. Signet en placard, with the Percy lion.

(fo. 39)
Myne owne goode Lorde ande broder, in my hartiest maner I commende me unto you, praying you to take the payn with my goode suster your bedfellowe to be with me at Morpeth on Sattreday next affore Shraftewsday, and that ye therof not faile, that we may make mery to geder the saide Shraftyd. And howe prousperously the Kynges affaires goeth forward here, your servant this berer can shewe you, to whome I pray you gyf credence. Written at my castell of Alnewike, the xxviijth day of January.

Your boundon faythffull
brother,
H. Northumbreland.

[Endorsed, fo. 39v] To myn owne goode Lorde ande broder, the Erle of Comberland.

33

Henry, sixth Earl of Northumberland, to the first Earl of Cumberland [*Undated; c.* 23 *August* 1533].

See introduction, p. 48. Northumberland here writes that Sir Thomas Wharton (later first Lord Wharton) is going up to the King to discover his pleasure concerning war or peace with Scotland. On 23 August 1533 Northumberland wrote from Newcastle to Cromwell that Wharton was going up to the King by the advice of the commissioners (these latter also occur in our letter) and will report to Cromwell on the 'occurents' in these parts (*L. & P.*, vi. 1019). At this moment the issue between war and peace was being debated, and in the event, as Northumberland here expects, a truce was concluded in the September. Cf. *ibid.*, 968, 1152, 1187.

Autograph.

(fo. 40)

Myn owne good Lord and brother, after my most harte recommendacion unto yow and to my derrest suster your bedffellow. Les[s] I cane not do acordyng unto my true and stedffast hart towardes yow than make yow (as hym that I compt me most bonden unto) partecipant off owr news here, the which ye shall mor at lynkth persave by the coppes off the Kynges letters unto me, my Lord Dacre and the comyssioners here. And wher at thys tym his Majeste doth wrytt unto yow for Cc men, to be in a redynes apon k[no]wleyge frome me had to repayre unto the Borders, I pray yow, my Lord, mak a good wysage ther off, thowgh I promes yow I looke for apeas and thynkyt werylye, wher for my openion hys ye shall be put your selff to no charge her in, for as I shall know, I shall not fale to satisffye yow with wayges. Sir Thomas Warton doth go upp from us all unto the Kynge, resoluttlye to know hys most gracius pleisur for war or peas, and that in post and haes[t]. My Lord, I commytt yow to God in hall hast, with the rude hand off

Your most boundon
faythfull brother,
H. Northumbreland.

[Endorsed, fo. 41v] [1] To myn owne goode Lord and brother, therle of Combreland.

[2] Lettres from my Lord of Northumberland.

(fos. 40v, 41, blank)

34

Henry, sixth Earl of Northumberland, to the first Earl of Cumberland, 12 *July* [? 1532].

See introduction, p. 47. The year 1532 seems all but certain. The more obvious terminal dates are 1532, before which Thomas Cromwell was not in a position to send Northumberland letters of the sort here mentioned, and 1536, since Northumberland died in June 1537. The King, we learn, had just summoned the Earl to London on some serious matter. I suggest that this concerned the supposed pre-contract between Northumberland and Anne Boleyn. In a quarrel with his wife, Northumberland asserted he had been betrothed to Anne; Lady Northumberland reported this in a letter to her father the Earl of Shrewsbury, who laid the matter before the Duke of Norfolk. In consequence, Northumberland was speedily brought to London and there before the Council denied that any pre-contract had existed; this denial he repeated before Archbishop Warham. These transactions were reported by Chapuys in a letter of 22 August 1532 (P. Friedmann, *Anne Boleyn*, i. 160-1 cites Vienna Archives P.C. 227, iv. fo. 57), and on 13 May 1536 Northumberland himself recalled them in a letter to Cromwell (*L.* & *P.*, x. 864). The visit to London is confirmed by a warrant which Northumberland granted at Hackney on 16 July (*L.* & *P.*, v. 1184), and no other visit has been discovered during the years 1532-6 about the month and day required by our letter. Topcliffe, where the Earl's grandfather had been murdered in April 1489, was perhaps the oldest home of the Percies in northern England; the manor house lay immediately to the W. of the motte-and-bailey castle of *c.* 1071. 'Prydow' is Prudhoe Castle, between Newcastle and Hexham, acquired by the family in 1392 and still in use at the time of this letter. Cf. Fonblanque, *op. cit.*, i. 539, and illustration at i. 385.
Autograph.

(fo. 42)
Myne owne good Lord and brothere, in my most harte maner I recommend me unto yow, with lyk thankes for the sendynge unto me my frend Jake your servant, by whom I do persie[v]e your good Lordsh[i]ppe to be contentyd, with my good Lady and suster, to myght me at Toplyff, assuryng yow that the kyndnes ther off hys not a lytyll to my comffortt, for the Kynge exceptyd, ye be the persons in the wordell [*sic*] I wold faynest se, and that my comffortt doth

rest in. And for the sertante ther off as yett by reson of this trubulsome wordell his unknow, as by my letters unto the Kynges Highnes ye shall persie[v]e, the coppes wher off I send yow, thynkyng never so longe to I speke with yow, in whom, as I have sayd, I have my most conffedens. And consernyng my goyng up, I send her with the coppes off my letters I resewyd from the Kynges Highnes and Mr Cromwell, praying yow, my good Lord, to have me recommendytt unto my good Lady and suster, whom above all [wohoman *cancelled*] women I dysiere most to be as natur byndytth me, trustyng ye wyll be mye excus for myn not wrytynge unto her at this tyme, for in good fayth, how I am troubled thys berer can show yow, as Our Lord knoyth, who kepp yow and send us more metyng shortly. At Prydow, the xij[th] day of July, with the rude hand off

Your bo[u]ndon and
most faythfull brother,
H. Northumberland.

[Endorsed, fo. 43v] To myn own good Lord and brother, my Lord off Combreland.

35

Lady Katherine Scrope to the first Earl of Cumberland,
14 *October* [1536].

See introduction, pp. 50-52. Sir James Metcalfe lived at Nappa, about five miles up Wensleydale beyond Bolton Castle. On 8 October the Earl of Cumberland had written a letter to him and other local gentlemen urging them to keep order in the dales (*L.* & *P.*, xi. 604). His son Christopher, here mentioned, subsequently married Katherine's younger sister Elizabeth Clifford (Whitaker, *Richmondshire*, i 406 and *infra*, p. 139). Richard Siggiswick lived at Walburn in Downholme parish, 3½ miles N. of Leyburn (*V.C.H., Yorks., North Riding*, i. 230 gives references). Richard survived till 1556, so cannot be identified with the aged Mr. Siggiswick who conducted a report-centre at Jervaulx for the Pilgrims (*L.* & *P.*, xii(1). 789). John, third Lord Latimer of Snape and husband of Katherine Parr (cf. *supra*, no. 6), was soon to be endangered by his rôle in the Pilgrimage. For references, see Dodds, index, s.v. Latimer. Sir

Christopher Danby of Thorpe Perrow, near Snape, Lord of Mashamshire and one of the co-heirs of the barony of Scrope of Masham, married Elizabeth, daughter of Richard, second Lord Latimer. Danby was taken by the commons and proceeded to play an important part in the Pilgrimage. For his life, see *Parliamentary Representation of the County of York*, ii (*Y.A.S. Rec. Ser.*, xcvi), pp. 14-5. George Bowes and his relatives surrendered Barnard Castle on 15 October and assumed command of the insurgents (Dodds, i. 202; *L. & P.*, xii(1). 775). On Helbeck Hall and Kettlewell, see *supra*, p. 51.

Autograph.

(fos. 42v, 43, blank)

(fo. 44)

My dewty promysed unto your Lordship in my most humbliest maner; advertysyng the same that yesterday the commons off Richmontshir did meat at Richmond, wher undoubtedly they dewydet them in thre partyes, whereoff one company there was commandet to come this day for my Lord my bedfelowe ore his litell boy & myn, Sir James Metcalff ore his sone Cristofer, & Richard Sigiswik, and to brynge them with them or elles to pull downe their housses and spoill them off their goodes. A nother company goth fore my Lord Latymer ore his sone, Mr. Danby, with other in thosse quarters. And the third company goth to Barnard Castell to bryng to them my cousyn George Bowes & his two uncles. My Lord my bedfelow is this nyght at Helbek Hall & wulbe with your Lordshipe at Skypton in as convenyent spead as he can maik, to tak suche parte as your Lordshipe dothe. And I wull come this mornyng towardes Katelwell & tary there off my bedfelowe, and wold come with hym to Skipton, iff ye thynk it good. And this nyght I have sent my litell boy with his nursse unto one poore mans housse, to be kept privy there to we knowe forther. And what your Lordshipes mynd is in the premysses I wull hertly besuche you to send it to Catelwell with this berere. Thus tholy Gost preserve youre good Lordship with my Lady my mother & all youres in comfort. At Bolton, this Setterday before day,

Your humbliest doughter,
Kateryn Scrope.

[Endorsed, fo. 44v] To the right honorabill & my veray good Lord and father, my Lord off Combreland.

36

Lady Katherine Cholmeley, alias *Scrope, to the third Earl of Cumberland,* 20 *June* [1583-1585].

See introduction, pp. 52-3. As there observed, the date of this letter must be between the burial of Katherine's second husband Sir Richard Cholmeley, 17 May 1583, and the death of her stepson Francis Cholmeley, 'about Pentecost 1586.' Richard Dutton of Whitby married her daughter Katherine Cholmeley (*Glover's Visitation*, p. 220). 'My cousin Mr. Manners' probably refers to one of the three younger sons, John, Roger and Thomas, of the first Earl of Rutland, who were all active in public life at this period. Their relationship to Katherine was remote: like her, they were descended from Thomas, fifth Lord Ros. The Clifford and Manners families were also distantly related by marriage through the Talbots. 'Mr. Crake' was probably Ralph Creyke of Marton and Cottingham, E. Yorks., living in 1584 and 1612 (*Glover's Visitation*, p. 163; J. Foster, *Yorkshire Pedigrees,* i). Sir William Fairfax was of the Steeton branch (*Glover's Visitation*, p. 97). Mr. Dalton probably belonged to the Hull and later Sleningford family, (*ibid*., p. 141; J. Foster, *Yorkshire Pedigrees,* i). 'Mr. Bethell' was probably Sir Hugh Bethel of Ellerton, surveyor to Queen Elizabeth in the East Riding (*ibid*.; *Glover's Visitation*, p. 241). 'My sonne Mr. Strangewiche' was Sir James Strangeways of Sneaton, who married the writer's step-daughter Margaret Cholmeley (*ibid*., p. 220). Katherine writes this letter from the home of one of her daughters: Barforth, 7 miles E. of Barnard Castle, where the manor and hall belonged to the Pudseys from the fifteenth to the seventeenth century (*V.C.H., Yorks., North Riding*, i. 68). This daughter Elizabeth Scrope married Thomas Pudsey and survived until 1620 (Clay, p. 201). The Cliffords had also a kinship with the Pudseys through the Shepherd Lord's second wife Florence Pudsey, who survived into the reign of Elizabeth. Cf. *infra*, p. 132.

The eighteenth-century endorsement is a nonsensical reading by some person ignorant of Tudor handwriting. Here the signature 'Scrope' resembles 'Dergy' only if read in terms of a modern hand.

Signed.

(fo. 45)

Right honorable, my dutie remembred. Your Lordshipp shall understand that at your beinge at London I sent unto my Ladie your wyffe for certiegen wrytinges which I put your L[ordship] in tryste withall, and now standinge nede[71] to have the same wrytinges, I require your L[ordship] to send them to me by this berer, my man Henrie Beareparke. I cannot as yet let your L[ordship] knowe how thinges shall fall out with me. Ther is certeigne gentlemen appoynted to ordre all thinges betwene me and my sonne Franncis Cholmeley, and also betwene him and my sonne Henrie, & my sonne Dutton. For the abydinge of the same ther ordre, I and my sonne Henrie & my sonne Dutton standes bounde unto my sonne Francis in five thousand poundes and he also standes bounde unto us in the same somme. For us ther ys appoynted my cousin Mr Manners, Mr Crake & Mr Spenser, and for my sonne Francis ys appointed Sir William Farefax, Mr Dalton, Mr Bethell and my sonne Mr Strangwiche. These are therfore to desyre your L[ordship] to wryte your lettre to my cousin Manners to wysshe him to be myndfull of our weightie causes, and further that he make no end without our consentes. Thus besechinge God to blesse your L[ordship] with muche increase of honnor, I reast, prainge your L[ordship] to make my humble commendacons to my good Ladye youre wyffe. Barfurthe, this xx[th] of June,

By your L[ordships] lovinge & assured aunte,
Catheryn Scrope.

[Endorsed, fo. 45v, in an eighteenth-century hand] From Catherine Dergy, perhaps Derby.

37

Henry, seventh Lord Scrope of Bolton, to the first Earl of Cumberland, 10 *August* [*c.* 1530].

See introduction, p. 33. About 1530, or possibly a little earlier, the writer's son John, later the eighth baron, married the Earl's eldest daughter Katherine Clifford, (G.E.C., xi. 547-8). This seems the only marriage between the families to which the present letter can allude. The seventh Lord Scrope died in or shortly before December 1533, since his son had livery of his lands on 29 December (*ibid.*).

The feast of St. Peter ad Vincula, when the Earl should have fulfilled

[71] 'Nede' interpolated.

his bargain, falls on 1 August. Fountains Abbey had not necessarily any direct rôle as custodian; while it is possible that the cups had been deposited there, Scrope's later remarks suggest that he now had them at Bolton. Though not on the most direct road between Skipton and Bolton, Fountains was easily accessible from both, and a reasonable rendezvous for the transaction of confidential business.

Signed.

(fo. 46)

Righte honorable and my verey goode Lorde, after my moste lowlie wyse I recomende me unto your goode Lordshipe. And where heretofore your Lordshipe pleasor was for to sende unto me two cuppes for to lie in plegge oonto the feaste of the Advincule of Saynt Peter last paste, for the somme of an hundreth powndes sterlinges; and then they to be redemyde by your Lordshipe, as appereth by a bill indented, maide betwix your saide Lordshipe and me off the saide cuppes, and day of payment also. So it was, my Lorde, accordinge to the tenor off the indentures of the covenantes of mariage, I sent two of my trusty servantes at the forsaide day of the Advincule unto Fontannce. And they gaff there attendance for to have received the same, and for to have delivered in my nayme acquittance for discharging of so moche money to your Lordshipe use. Albeit, my Lorde, I well perceivede by my saide servantes ther came none frome your Lordshipe at the saide day so lymitted. Wheroff, my Lord, I dyd marvell, supposinge unto me that your Lordshipe had some gret besynes uppon hande at that day, so as it was out of your remembrannce. In consideracion of which premisses to be accompleshed by your saide Lordshipe, it may nowe eftsones please youre goode Lordshipe for to send unto me by your Lordshipe trusty servanntes the forsaid hundreth powndes in good and lawfull payment. Whiche so doon, your Lordshipe shall have delivered to the handes of your said trusty servantes not onelie your Lordshipe two cuppes in saiftie, but also aquittance subscribed with myne owne hande for discharging of the saide hundreth powndes, as knowith our Lorde Jhesus, who evermore have your goode Lordshipe in his blissed tuicion. Att Bolton, the xth day of Auguste,

Youre assured
Herre Scrop.

[Endorsed, fo. 46v] To the righte honorable and my veray good Lord, the Erle of Cumberland.

38

Henry, seventh Lord Scrope of Bolton, to the first Earl of Cumberland [*Undated; ? c.* 1530-1533].

See introduction, p. 49. It so happens that much of the background to this dispute can be supplied. The Wiberghs had been landowners in the parish of Clifton, Westmorland, since the time of Edward III. In 1526-7 one Thomas Wibergh held Clifton manor of the first Earl of Cumberland. Ten years later, the Earl made an award between our Thomas Wibergh and Sir John Lowther of Lowther, Westmorland, who disputed Wibergh's right to enclose certain lands. By this award the Earl allowed Wibergh to keep these lands enclosed (Nicholson and Burn, i. 417-8). The interesting fact then emerges that Anne Wibergh, the servant of Lady Scrope, was not only the wife of Thomas (which our letter does not make clear) but also a Lowther and a niece of the Earl, since the latter's sister Dorothy had married Hugh Lowther, father of Anne and son of Sir John Lowther; cf. *Pedigrees . . . of Cumberland and Westmorland*, ed. J. Foster, pp. 84, 148. Anne and her husband were at the time of this letter still quite young: she had a brother born as late as 1532. Theirs may well have been a child-marriage followed by a dispute between the families over the young wife's lands. The mention of the Duke of Richmond's Council makes the letter not earlier than 1525; the fact that it was written by Henry Lord Scrope gives the terminal date December 1533. A time towards the end of this period seems indicated. Though the Lowthers and the Wiberghs continued in dispute, the young couple must ultimately have come together: at all events, they had a son who married a sister of Archbishop Edmund Grindal (*ibid*., p. 148).
Signed.

(fo. 47)
My verrey goode Lorde, in my most lovynge maner I recommende me unto you. Plesse it youre goode Lordshipe to knowe that one Anne Wybere, which is servantt to my wyff, hath hade certen londis to hir feoffement of hyr husbondes, accordynge to the covenanntes of theyre maraige, & hath contenuede & injoyede the same pesible to this Martynmes, that she is interuppitt by one Thomas Wybere, whiche I suppose doth belonge youre Lor[d]shyppe. She wold have putt in hir bill of complant affor my Lord of Richmonde's counsell, which I wold not one belongynge me shuld do affor youre

Lordshyppe plessor were knowne therin, seynge the contrary parte[72] is under youre rewell. Wherfor yf it wyll lyke your Lordshipe that she have hir rentt & an awnswere hym as the lawe wyll, then she wyll seke for no fordere remedy, wher in I will dissyer your Lordshyppe to be goode lorde, & that I may knowe your plessor how she shalbe orderitt in the same. And so the Holy Gost have your goode Lordshippe in his kepynge.

Youres assuerdly,
Herre Scrop.

[Endorsed, fo. 47v] To my verrey goode Lord, my Lorde of Combberland, be thes bil deliverede.

39

John, eighth Lord Scrope of Bolton, to the [? *first*] *Earl of Cumberland, 23 February* [?1534-1542].

John succeeded his father in December 1533, was summoned to Parliament from 5 January 1534 until 5 January 1549; he died on 22 June 1549. The phraseology of the present letter bears a close resemblance to that of nos. 40, 41, 42 and hence suggests that he was writing to the first Earl, his father-in-law. The hand is the same as that of no. 40, dated 1540. It is, however, just possible that the addressee could have been the second Earl. The editor has so far failed to discover records of the suit *Waller v. Morlande*, which should yield a more precise date.

Winton, a township in the parish of Kirkby Stephen, belonged to the Clifford estates (*Y.A.J.*, xviii. 371; Nicholson and Burn, i. 547). Edward Waller was no doubt an ancestor of Thomas Waller, the yeoman who founded the school at Kaber nearby and died in 1689 (*ibid.*, i. 551). Thomas's relative Robert Waller, who granted lands in trust to this school in 1681, is described as a yeoman of Winton (*ibid.*, i. 548).

Signed.

(fo. 48)
Right honorable and my veray goode Lorde, in my right homeble wyse I recommende me unto youre goode Lordshipe, and wull

[72] Party.

right so desyer the sayme to be goode lorde unto one Edwarde Waller, the berer hereof, as concernyng one parcell of a tenement in Wynton of your Lordeshipe is lande, nowe in traves betwyxt the saide Edwarde Waller and one Morlande of Wynton afforesaide; and the rather at this my request. And thus I besuche Jhesu to preserve youre goode Lordeshipe in honour to his pleasoure. Wrytten at my castell at Bolton, the xxiijth day of February,

Your Lordshypes assurede
Jhon Scrope.

[Endorsed, fo. 48v] To the right honorable and my veray goode Lorde, my Lorde of Combrelande, delyver this.

40

John, eighth Lord Scrope of Bolton, to the first Earl of Cumberland, 11 *April* [1540 *or* 1541].

See introduction, p. 34. This item is closely linked with no. 41: in the original MS they have been bound in reverse order. On the Metcalfes of Nappa, see also no. 35. This family rose to importance in Wensleydale in the last two decades of the fifteenth century, when Thomas Metcalfe waxed wealthy as crown surveyor of Middleham and the Richmond liberties. Cf. W. C. and G. Metcalfe, *Metcalfe Records* (1891), pp. 36-7. His heir James served as High Sheriff of Yorkshire in 1525 and was knighted in 1528: having made further extensions of the family estates, he died in 1539 (ibid., pp. 48-63). He was succeeded by his son Christopher, the subject of these letters, who married Elizabeth, third daughter of the first Earl of Cumberland. Christopher and his adversary, the eighth Lord Scrope, were hence brothers-in-law, while the Earl's position between them must have proved somewhat embarrassing. In 1534 Christopher had purchased the reversion of his father's offices and he is described in the patent as master forester of Wensleydale, parker of Woodhall and Wanless, and supervisor of Middleham (*ibid.*, pp. 78-9, citing Pat. 25 Hen. VIII, pt. 1). In 1536 Lord Scrope obtained a patent nominating himself as bailiff of Richmond, steward of the liberty, master forester within the liberties of Richmond and constable of the castles of Richmond and Middleham. To these offices an annual wage of £50 was attached (Metcalfe, *op. cit.*, p. 79, citing Pat. 37 Hen. VIII, pt. 1).

Immediately on the death of Sir James Metcalfe, Scrope challenged Christopher's right to the latter's offices, which obviously overlapped with those now claimed by Scrope. Christopher thereupon instituted a Star Chamber suit against him. Of this suit we have only fragmentary records, consisting of the depositions of Scrope's witnesses (Metcalfe, *op. cit.*, pp. 79-80 outlines Star Chamber Proc., bdle. 8, no. 344). Though no decree has survived, the paramount jurisdiction of Scrope was at some stage upheld, since Christopher surrendered his letters patent *quoad officium magistri forestarii sive magistri deductus ferarum infra forestas de Wensleydale, Radale et Bishopdale*. This surrender was taken at Skipton on 15 April 1542 before Henry Earl of Cumberland and Sir Thomas Tempest (Metcalfe, *op. cit.*, pp. 80-1, from a marginal note in Pat. 25 Hen. VIII, pt. 1).

Our new documents show a phase of this dispute unknown to the learned editors of the *Metcalfe Records*. The Lord Privy Seal, it now transpires, referred the matter to a northern commission. In letter 40, dated 11 April, Scrope asks Cumberland to induce his two fellow-commissioners Sir William Babthorpe and Robert Challoner K.C. (Councillors in the North, respectively 1525-1555, and 1530-1555) to come out to Middleham before Whitsunday to hear the case. He also forwards a letter from the Lord Privy Seal directed to Cumberland alone, declaring his Lordship's views on the matter. This energetic personal intervention seems distinctly characteristic of Thomas Cromwell. Even more interestingly, Scrope here urges Cumberland to keep the dealings with the Lord Privy Seal secret from the Lord President of the North, Robert Holgate (then Bishop of Llandaff), and from Sir Robert Bowes (Councillor in the North, 1525-1555), who were special friends and great favourers of Christopher Metcalfe.

In letter 41, dated 6 June, Scrope tells Cumberland that Babthorpe and Challoner want to sit in York; he apologises in that Cumberland will thus be drawn so far from home, and reveals that he is also paying the expenses for bringing forty other witnesses to York. No. 41 proves the matter to be indeed a stage of the dispute we have outlined, since Scrope sends Cumberland a dossier of the documents demonstrating his own right to the master forestership of all the parks and chases of Richmondshire. The date of these letters must thus be 1540 or 1541; it cannot be 1542, since Christopher had surrendered his claims by 15 April in that year. If this Lord Privy Seal be indeed Cromwell, the date must be 1540, because Cromwell lost his appointments on 10 June 1540, the Privy Seal being transferred to the first Earl of Southampton four days later (*Handbook of British Chronology*, 2nd edn., p. 93).

To avoid confusion, it should here be noticed that a different dispute was raging contemporaneously between Lord Scrope and Christopher Metcalfe. In November 1539 the former began a Chancery suit challenging the latter's claim to Nappa itself. This led to litigation even more complex and protracted; it is described in remarkable detail in the *Metcalfe Records*, pp. 81 *seqq*., but has only background relevance to our own two letters. 'My cousyn Gascone' in no. 41 should be Sir William Gascoigne of Gawthorpe (cf. no. 7 *supra*) or his son William, who was aged about 39 at this time (J. Foster, *Yorkshire Pedigrees*, i). I observe no closer relationship than that Sir William's mother, Scrope's grandmother, and Scrope's wife's mother were all Percies, though of different generations.

Signed.

(fo. 50)

Right honorable and my synguler goode Lorde, in my hartieste wyse I recommende me unto youe. And by this berere my servante I do sende a lettre directede to youe and other commyssioners frome the Lorde Privey Seall concernyng the mattere in traves betwyxt me and Christofer Metcalf, requyrynge your Lordshipe that eyther it wull please youe by your lettre, to be wrytten to the other comyssyoners, to appoynt suche day at Midelhame as your Lordshipe shall thynke convenyent before Whitsonday, or ells by your saide lettre to knowe of Maistere Babthorpe and Maister Challonere by theyr wrytynge whan they can be at sufficient laysour for the saide matter, before and of thissyde the saide feaste of Whitsonday. And if it shall please youe to sende the saide Lord Privey Sealle is lettre to the other comyssyoners, that than we wolde in your saide lettre requyer theme not to shewe the saide orde Privey Seall is lettre to my Lorde Presydent ne to Mr. Bowis, bycause they be speciall freyndes and grete favorers to the saide Christofer Metcalf. Also I do sende by this berer my servante an other lettere directede to youe allone frome the saide Lorde Privey Seall, wherin I thynke ye shall knowe his Lordshippes pleasoure in the saide matter betwyxt me and the saide Christofer Metcalf. And thus I besuche Jhesu ever[73] preserve youre goode Lordshipe in muche honoure longe to endure. Wryttyn at my castell at Bolton, the xjth[74] day off Aprill,

Your Lordshipes owne assurede
Jhon Scrope.

[Endorsed, fo. 51v] To the right honorable and my veray goode Lorde the Erle of Comebrelande yeve this.

(fos. 50v, 51, blank)

[73] 'Ever' is repeated.

[74] Replacing 'xiijth', which has been cancelled.

41

John, eighth Lord Scrope of Bolton, to the first Earl of Cumberland, 6 June [1540 *or* 1541].

See the note to no. 40 *supra.*
Signed.

(fo. 49)
Right honorabill, & my veray good Lord, in my hertiest wisse I commend me unto your good Lordship, and doth perceiwe by my servantt that youre Lordship hath receiwed a lettre from Mr. Babthorpe & Mr Chaloner, that they ere contented to sitt uppon the commyssion at York the next Monday. My Lord, I am weray sory to putt you & my cousyn Gascone to suche charges in rydyng so ferre off, & also itt shalbe no litell charge to me, bryngyng xl[ti] witnesses to York uppon my party. Wherfor I have sentt unto youre Lordship all suche specialties as maketh for me for the masterforstershipe of all the parkes & chaices in Richmondshire, desyryng youre Lordship to luk uppon the same; and as ye thynk that I shall doy in the premysses, I will requyre your Lordshipe to ascerteyn me agayn by my chapleyn this berer, unto whom I pray you yewe credence. And thus tholy Gost kepe you. Att my castell off Bolton, this vj[th] day off June,

Your lordship owne assurede
Jhon Scrope.

[Endorsed, fo. 49v.] To the right honorabul and my varey good Lord, my Lord off Combreland.

42

John Scrope, later eighth Lord Scrope of Bolton, to the first Earl of Cumberland, 30 *October* [?1533].

See introduction. p. 50. This letter was written during the lifetime of the writer's father, Henry, seventh Lord Scrope, who died in or shortly before December 1533 (*supra*, no. 37). For obvious reasons 30 October 1533 seems the most likely date when the son would act for his sick father in relation to an important legal dispute. William Thoresby died in 1528; the dates of his successors suggest that a minority may have occurred about this time (*V.C.H., Yorks., North Riding*, i. 209). Some time before our letter was written, there had been previous enquiries into the wardship. The commissioners here mentioned were flourishing c. 1533. On Sir Robert Bowes see *supra*, no. 40, where his hostility to the Scropes is again shown. Ralph Evers (Eure) may have been either the grandfather or the grandson; both were soon to figure as opponents of the Pilgrimage of Grace. John Norton was John Conyers, *alias* Norton, who owned Norton Conyers, Gilling and other manors, was aged 40 in 1520 and died in 1556 (J. Foster, *Yorkshire Pedigrees*, ii). 'John Barton' is probably John Bretton, deputy secretary to the King's Council in the North 1527-42 (Reid, p. 488; *L. & P.*, iv(2). 4042). Edmund Copendale (Coppyndale, etc.) came of an armigerous family of Beverley and Hull, (*Test. Ebor.*, iv. 7-8) and occurs as J.P. in the East Riding as early as 1530-3 (*L. & P.*, iv, v, vi, indices). In the Pilgrimage of Grace he was a reputed loyalist, who fled to Scarborough Castle, yet bought the lead of Marton Priory from Robert Aske (*ibid.*, xii(1). 392, p. 186; 698(2)). The present editor does not know the date at which he became a feodary, but it was probably in his official capacity that he was disputing the Thoresby wardship with the Scropes. On the functions of feodaries see H. E. Bell, *The Court of Wards and Liveries*, pp. 38 *seqq.*

John Scrope writes this letter from Langley, 5½ miles N. of Durham, where the castellated mansion belonged to the Scropes. Surtees (*Durham*, ii. 332-3) describes in detail the Scrope inscriptions dating from this same period on the mantelpiece of the great hall.

The notion at first occurred to the editor that our letter might conceivably have been written in the late forties by Scrope's eldest son, also called John. This youth, born after 1530, predeceased his father, who died on 22 June 1549 (N. H. Nicolas, *The Controversy between Sir Richard Scrope and Sir Robert Grosvenor*, ii. 62). But the possibility of his authorship, already rather remote, is excluded by the fact that the younger Sir Ralph Evers was killed at Ancrum Moor on 6 March 1545, when this younger John Scrope was still in his early teens.

Signed.

(fo. 52)

Right honorable, and my veray good Lorde, in my most homble wise I recommend me unto your good Lordship. Pleasith the sayme to be advertised that our adversaris hayth brought downe a commyssion to inquer agayne of the wardship of Thursby. My Lorde, this matter ys only wrought uppon mallece. And the commissioneres be Robert Bowys, Rawfe Everes, Johne of Norton and Johne Barton. And thay syt of the sayme uppon Munday next at Thirske; which commissioneres be nether favorable ne indeferent to my Lord my father. Wold yt therefor please your goode Lordship to writ a lettre to Roberte Bowyse and a nother to Edmund Coppyndayll, the Kynges feodory, which ys our adversary, advertesyng thayme bothe not to be so extreyme and parshalle agaynst my Lorde my father right, with sum quyk clawsys of your Lordshipes mynd, as ye thinke good. And that yt wold please your Lordship to sende one of your Lordshipes owne servanntes with your letteres. Forther, my Lorde, I homble besuche your Lordship to be good lorde unto my Lorde my fathers servannte, this berer naymyde Gyfflot [*sic*] Gylpyng, in such causys as he wull ascerten your Lordship of, yf yt wull please you to yeve hym audience. So I besuch Jesu ever preserve your goode Lordship in honor to hys pleasor. Wryttyn at Langley, the penult. of Octobre,

Your Lordshipes own
at comm[an]dment,
John Scrope.

[Endorsed, fo. 52v] To the right honorable and my veray good Lord, my Lord of Cumbrland, be this d[elivere]d.

43

Edward, third Earl of Derby, to the first Earl of Cumberland, 29 August [1536].

See introduction, pp. 30-31. In 1890 a version of this letter was printed from a copy belonging to Miss Farington of Norden Hall, Lancashire, in *The Correspondence of Edward Earl of Derby* (*Chetham Soc., new ser.*, xix. 127, no. 61). It is there headed 'To the Erle of Northumberland': surely in error, since it appears unlikely that Northumberland could also have been laying claim to the stewardship of Winterburn. The confusion probably arose from the fact that in another letter of the same collection (p. 114, no. 47), Derby did refer to a claim by Northumberland to a stewardship of Furness Abbey; yet this was to the stewardship, not of Winterburn, but of lands in Borrowdale. The verbal variants of the Chetham

Society version are noted below, but they possess little significance. In 1535 both Derby and Cumberland are shown as stewards of Furness. The former received a fee of £10 for exercising the office *in comitatibus Eboraci et Lancastrie*; the latter £6 for acting as steward *de Wynterburne* (*Valor Eccles.*, v. 270).

The present letter contains no precise evidence as to the year, but the copy printed by the Chetham Society is headed 'Litter[e] misse A[nn]o xxviii H[enrici] VIII', and the year 1536 would cause the letter to fit easily into the story of Furness. On the efforts of Cumberland to extract the lease of Winterburn from Furness, see no. 3 *supra.*

Signed.

(fo. 53)

My vere good lord and cosyn, in my right herty and loving maner I commend me to you. And wher as the abbot and covent of the monastery of Furnes have made me their stward of all their landes belonging to their monastery, as may appere by their[75] writing under their covent seale; And that notwithstanding, as I am informed, ye pretend to be stward unto the said abbot of his lordship of Wynterburn,[76] and by the color of the same your pretence do not[77] only punysshe the said abbotes tenantes their and do order them lyke as and ye were their stward[78] in dede, whiche is unknown to me that ye shuld have any suche interest soo to do. Wherfor in my moost herty and loving maner, I desir you that ye will no forther intermedell therin unto suche tym your right be proved to be better than myn. And that known, I shall not only be contented that ye shall have and injoye that that[79] ye ought to have of right, but also be contented[80] that they shalbe reformed and punyshed, if they have offended you or any of yours; desiring you to be good lord unto the said tenantes upon their demeanors, and the better at my request; and that I maye be ascerteyned by writing of your mynd herin. At[81] thus hertly fare ye well. At my manor of Knowseley, the xxix day of August,

Your lovyng cosyn,
E. Derby.

[75] *Chetham Soc.* omits 'their'.
[76] *C.S.*: 'Wenterburn'.
[77] *C.S.*: 'ye do not'.
[78] *C.S.*: 'ye were stward their [*sic*].
[79] *C.S.*: omits second 'that'.
[80] *C.S.*: 'also to be content'.
[81] *Sic* for 'And'. *C.S.*: 'herin, and thus rest. Knowesley, the xxix day,' etc.

[Endorsed, fo. 53v] To my [right welbiloved, *cancelled*] vere good Lord cosyn, the Erle of Cumberland, be this delyvered.

44

Eleanor, Countess of Cumberland, to the second Earl of Cumberland, 14 February [1543-1547].

See introduction, p. 54. This letter is not with the rest in B.M. Additional MS 48965. It was formerly with Lord Hothfield's records at Appleby Castle, but at some date more than a quarter of a century ago, it appears to have been removed from the muniment room. Its present whereabouts remains unknown (letter of Capt. Fordyce, 9 April 1957, to Yorks. Archaeol. Soc.). It had, however, been photographed about 1916, and a tiny copy inserted in one corner of plate 3 in Dr. G. C. Williamson's *Lady Anne Clifford* (1922). In itself almost illegible, this copy has been subjected to magnification, and our present version is at least tolerably exact. Dr. Williamson in his brief mention of the letter (*ibid.*, p. 22) supplies the endorsement; in his list of illustrations he dates it 1540, but this cannot be correct. Eleanor certainly wrote this at Carlton after her husband's succession to the Earldom: 14 February 1543 is the earliest possible date and 14 February 1547 the latest, since she died at Brougham in November 1547 (*infra,* p. 144). I observe no certain dating-clues in the known movements of the Earl, but one of his few extant letters from these years was written at Carlton on 16 February 1545 (*L.* & *P.*, xx(1). 207): it is not impossible that he returned to his wife immediately on receipt of this present alarming letter. Dr. Williamson refers to this as an autograph letter, but the point is not self-evident. Eleanor's signature is in a regular Italian script, very different from the rather untidy hand of the body of the letter.

Regarding the nature of Lady Eleanor's illness, it always remains difficult to base an opinion on retrospectively described symptoms. A medical colleague suggests, however, that her complaints and her known heavy build, would make a gall-stone impacted in the common bile-duct a possible diagnosis; from this condition complications sufficiently severe to cause death could easily arise.

'Doctor Stephyns' may well be Stephen Thomson,[82] formerly physician to the sixth Earl of Northumberland, who had rewarded his services by

[82] 'Dr Stephyns' was, e.g., often applied to Stephen Gardiner.

an extensive lease of Percy properties in York (Fonblanque, *op. cit.*, i. 407, n. 2; *L. & P.*, xii(2). 57). Somewhat less likely is Stephen Tubley M.D., who occurs in York records for a few years before his death in 1558 (*Y.A.S. Rec. Ser.*, xiv. 167; cx. 122, 172). Eleanor's visitor was her sister Anne, wife of Edward Grey, third Lord Powys. Carlton was one of the manors recently acquired by her father-in-law. The Cliffords had there a house and park called Newbiggin, one of those subsequently repaired by Lady Anne Clifford (*Craven*, p. 223).

Signed.

Jhesus

Dere hart, after my moste hartye commendatyons, thys shalbe to sertify yow that sense yowr departure frome me, I have byn very seke & att thys present my watter ys very redd, wherby I suppos I have the jaundes & the aygew both, for I have none abyde to meate & I have suche payns in my syde & towardes my bak as I had att Brauham, wher ytt be gane with me furst. Wher for I desyre yow to help me to a physyssyon & that thys berer may brynge hym with hym, for now in the begynning I trust I may have gud remedy, & the longer ytt ys delayed the worse ytt wylbe. Also my sister Powys ys comyd to me & ys very desyrous to se yow, whiche I trust shalbe the sooner at this tyme & thus Jhesu send hus both healthe. Att my lodge of Carleton, the xiiij[th] day of February.

And, dere hart, I pray yow send for Doctor Stephyns, for he knowyth best my complexon for such cawsys.

By yowr assuryd loufyng wyff,
Elenor Cumbarland.

[Endorsed] To my mooste lovynge Lorde and husband, the Erle of Combreland.

APPENDIX

A SUMMARY OF THE LIVES OF THE VETERIPONTS, CLIFFORDS, ETC., BY ANNE CLIFFORD, COUNTESS OF PEMBROKE [BRITISH MUSEUM, HARLEY MS. 6177, pp. 74-92]

In this appendix we print only that section of Lady Anne Clifford's account of her ancestors which is strictly relevant to the foregoing letters. It covers the lives, marriages and children of the Shepherd Lord, and of the first two Earls of Cumberland: from this point onwards the remainder of the manuscript happens already to be print.[1] This Harley manuscript is one of several copies and abridgements made from the 'Great Books' compiled under Lady Anne's personal supervision. The three versions of these 'Great Books', each bound in three volumes, have been described by Dr. Williamson, who supposed our present manuscript to be taken from the version at Appleby Castle, though it is not in fact quite identical with any of the three.[2]

The whole manuscript is entitled, 'A Summary of the lives of the Veteriponts, Cliffords, and Earls of Cumberland, and of the Lady Anne, Countess Dowager of Pembroke, Dorsett and Montgomery etc. daughter and heir to George Clifford, Earl of Cumberland, in whom the name of the said Cliffords determined. Copied from the original manuscript the 29th of December 1737 by Henry Fisher.'[3]

Though diffuse, slow-moving and in detail repetitive, this compilation remains a basic document for the lives of the Cliffords during the Tudor period. Only here and there does mere hearsay family tradition obtrude itself, for the greater part of the work is based upon inquisitions *post mortem*, deeds, family letters and other record sources, to which the compiler several times alludes in the course of the extract printed below. However enthusiastic her antiquarianism, Lady Anne's study of family history had also derived from sterner necessities. From 1605 to 1643, first her mother, and then Anne herself,

[1] *Lives of Lady Anne Clifford*, pp. 1 *seqq.*

[2] G. C. Williamson, *Lady Anne Clifford*, p. 363; for other manuscripts deriving from the 'Great Books' see *Lives of Lady Anne Clifford*, pp. xi-xii.

[3] Dr. Williamson seems to have known nothing concerning this copyist, whom the present editor has also hitherto failed to trace.

were engaged in intermittent proceedings against her father's heirs male, who had assumed not only the Earldom, but also—wrongfully as it came to be proved—the barony of Clifford, the family estates and the hereditary sheriffwick of Westmorland.[4] These finally came to her on 11 December 1643 with the death of her cousin Henry, the fifth Earl, and she proceeded to enjoy her inheritance until her death in 1676. The chief purpose of the 'Great Books' was to amass materials which would carry weight in the lawcourts.[5] The frequent self-regarding references to Anne's own heritage and position remind us that she had good reason to prosecute her researches with accuracy.

The introduction to our letters owes not a little to the following text; in turn, it often suffices to explain the latter and subsequent annotation may be limited to those matters not already covered.

[p. 74, fo. 38v] A Summary of the Records of Henry Lord Clifford, 14th Hereditary High Sheriff & Baron of Westmoreland, & 10th Lord of the Honor of Skypton in Craven & Baron Vesey,[6] whose first Wife was Anne St. John, Cosen Germain by the half blood to King Henry the 7th, and his 2d Wife was Mrs Florence Pudsey.

This Henry Lord Clifford was born in the year 1454, the year before his grandfather Thomas lord Clifford was slain, & he was betwixt 6 & 7 years old when his own father John Lord Clifford was slain, the 28th or 29th day of March[7] in Anno Domini 1461, the first year of Edward the 4th. And tho this Henry Clifford was so young at his fathers death, yet was he not admitted to be a ward to the King, by reason that presently after his fathers death, he & all his posterity were attainted of high treason by Act of Parliament for adhering to the house of Lancaster & for killing the Earl of Rutland, & all their lands both in Craven & Westmoreland and other places, were either given away or kept in the Kings custody all his reign, and his brother Richard the 3d's Reign after him, but restitution thereof was made by Act of Parliament to this Henry Lord Clifford & his heirs, the first year of Henry the 7th. In which time of his attainder, from the 1st of Edward the 4th to the 1st of Henry the 7th, he was miracu-

[4] For a summary of the situation see G.E.C., iii. 295-6.

[5] G. C. Williamson, *op. cit.*, p. 359.

[6] *Sic*. Cf. *infra*, p. 132, n. 26.

[7] In fact on 28 March, the day before Towton.

lously preserved in an obscure manner amongst shepherds in several places in Yorkshire & Cumberland, during that time, which was some 24 years.[8] Which said Henry Lord Clifford after his restitution lived possessor of his lands & honors 37 years and upwards, & he lived to be a very rich man.

He dyed the 23d of April 1523, the 15th year of Henry the 8th, he being then by computation about 69 or 70 years old at the time of his death, & by his last will and testament he appointed his dead body to be buryed in White Fryars by his grandfather Henry Bromflett Lord Vesey,[9] within the suburbs of London, or if he dyed in the North that his body should be buried either in the Abby of Shap in Westmoreland or in Bolton Abby in Craven, & certain it is he dyed in the North, & undoubtedly he was buried in one of those 2 abbys, for he was a great benefactor to both. And he was the 1st Lord Clifford of Westmoreland & Skypton who married a 2d wife & was never beyond the seas, or abroad in the wars, save only in the armys that were sent into Scotland by King Henry the 7th and Henry 8th with other noble men, in most [p. 75, fo. 39] of which he was always present.

Of his first Wife

His first wife was Anne St. John, only daughter of Sir John St. John of Bletsoe, and only sister to Sir John St. John his son, and by the half blood she was cosin germain to King Henry the 7th, for her father was half brother to that Kings mother, Margaret Countess of Richmond & Derby, which King as it is thought did restore the said Lord to his lands & honors & estate, the rather because he did then marry that cosin germain of his.

For though the said King favoured him, because of his father and grandfather were slain in the service of the house of Lancaster, yet by tradition it is received, that the cause chiefly why he recovered his lands and honours was because he married the said Kings cosin german, Anne St. John.

This Anne St. John, Lady Clifford, of whom we now treat, was a woman of great goodness, piety & devotion, and lived for the most part a country life in her husbands castles in the North, during the

[8] Somewhat questionable, in view of the pardon of 1472. Cf. *supra*, p. 19.

[9] Lord Vescy's will, proved 31 January 1469, stipulates that he shall be buried in the church of the Whitefriars, London (*North Country Wills, Surtees Soc.*, cxvi. 53).

time she lived his wife, which was about 21 years. This wife of his was so great an housewife, as that she caused tapistry hangings, which was then a rare thing here in England, to be made, & some of them are remaining untill this time, with the arms of her self & husband wrought in them.[10]

But towards her latter end, her husband was unkind to her, & had 2 or 3 children (base) by another woman, so as by reason of that & of her husbands taking part with some of the Commons about taxes against the said King Henry the 7th in the latter end of his reign, he was in some disgrace with the said King.[11] And by the charter of the Prior of Gisborne[12] it appears this excellent & virtuous Lady Anne St. John, Lady Clifford, was alive the 12th of May, in the 21st year of Henry the 7th, but certain it is, she dyed within a while after, & her dead body was buried in the vault of Skypton church in Craven.

Their Children

Henry Clifford their eldest son was born A.D. 1493 & lived after to enjoy his fathers lands & honors about 19 years, & he was about 2 years & almost 3 months after his fathers decease created first of all Earl of Cumberland by King Henry 8th in the Palace of Bridewell in London, the 18th day of June in the year 1525, the 17th of that Kings reign; so as he lived Earl of Cumberland 17 years, wanting some two months. He was about 30 years old when his father dyed, as appears by inquisitions, [p. 76, fo. 39v] and himself this Henry first Earl of Cumberland dyed the 22d of April in 1542, about the 34 year of Henry the 8th.

Thomas Clifford the 2d son married Lucy, daughter to Sir Anthony Brown Kt.,[13] but he & she dyed without issue. He was Governor of

[10] The inventory of tapestries at Skipton in 1572 seems to describe some of these: i.e., 'Item a v piece hangynge of red, white and other colers, with armes, xxxiii s. iiijd' (*Craven*, p. 401).

[11] This phrase is repeated *infra*, p. 135, with the addition that in 21 Henry VII (1505-6) he was called upon to prove his title to his Westmorland lands and his sheriffwick. The actual records of this *quo warranto* had been used to prove Lady Anne's own rights. This is probably a more solid fact than his alleged support of the Commons' resistance to taxation. Nevertheless, the latter story acquires a little more plausibility when it is recalled that 1504 was the year when the Commons, led by More, are said by Roper to have resisted the royal claim to feudal aids. Cf. E. E. Reynolds, *Saint Thomas More*, pp. 57-9.

[12] Guisborough.

[13] Cf. on 'Dame Lucye Clifford,' *Y.A.J.*, xviii. 374.

Berwick Castle, & had many other places of trust & imployments conferred upon him by King Henry the 8th.

Mabel Clifford their eldest daughter marryed to William Fitz-Williams Earl of Southampton,[14] by whom he had two sons that lived to be men, but they both dyed without issue before him & himself dyed the 34th year of Henry the 8th at Newcastle in Tyne without issue,[15] leaving his half brother by the mothers side, Anthony Browne, his heir; which Anthony Browne was father to the first Viscount Monntacute; & the foresaid Mabel also dyed without issue;[16] & this William FitzWilliams & Mabel his wife were the chief renewers & repairers of Cowdry House in Sussex, wherein their arms were set up in stone in many places.[17]

Eleanor Clifford, 2d daughter & 4th child, married to Markenfield.[18]

Anne Clifford, 3d daughter and 5th child, was married to Robert Metcalf, from whom the family of the Metcalfs are descended.[19]

Joan Clifford, 4th daughter & 6th child, was marryed to Sir Ralph Bowes of Areton,[20] from whom the Bowes in Yorkshire are descended.

Hir 2d Wife and Children by her

His 2d wife was Mrs. Florence Pudsey, daughter to Mr [*blank*]

[14] In November 1513. Lady Mabel was one of Queen Katherine's gentlewomen. Cf. G.E.C., xii(1). 121.

[15] On 15 October 1542, while leading the van of the army into Scotland (*ibid., loc. cit.*).

[16] At Farnham, where she was buried 1 Sept. 1550 (*Machyn's Diary*, p. 2).

[17] These armorial devices were a prominent feature of the house, which was destroyed by fire in 1793. Cf. J. Timbs and A. Gunn, *Abbeys, Castles and Ancient Halls*, iii. 374.

[18] Sir Ninian Markenfield of Markenfield Hall, near Ripon.

[19] The Anne Clifford who, as widow of Robert Clifton, wrote Letter 23 *supra*. Lady Anne evidently knew nothing of her marriage to Clifton, and may well be mistaken in this reference to a marriage with Robert Metcalfe. *Infra*, p. 139, she correctly notes the marriage of Anne's niece Elizabeth to Sir Christopher Metcalfe, using similar phraseology. But the meticulous *Metcalfe Records* contain no Robert who could have married Anne, and make no mention of her in relation to any member of the Metcalfe family. In *Glover's Visitation*, p. 409, Sir Christopher's brother Edward (*recte* Edmund) is married to 'Anne daughter of —— Clifton', but both he and his younger brother Robert were born after 1520. Cf. *Metcalfe Records*, p. 62 and pedigree at p. 1.

[20] Airton, near Settle. He was of the well-known Streatlam family; cf. *Glover's Visitation*, p. 597.

Pudsey,[21] by whom this Henry Lord Clifford had 2 or 3 sons that dyed very young, and one daughter Dorothy Clifford, who was marryed to Sir Hugh Lowther of Lowther in Westmoreland,[22] from whence the Lowthers of that county are descended; so as Sir John Lowther Kt. & Bart. there is the 5th in lineal descent from the said Hugh & Dorothy Clifford his wife. And it is to be noted, that her husbands mother was that Anne Thirkeld who was daughter to Sir Lancelot Thirkeld by John Lord Clifford's widdow the Lady Vesey, so as this Dorothy & her husband were cosin germans by the half blood to one another. This Florence, widdow to Henry Lord Clifford, did marry for her 2d husband Richard Lord Gray,[23] one of the younger sons of Thomas [first *interpolated*] Lord Marquess of Dorsett[24] of that family. She outlived him also some years, & she was an old woman when she dyed, [p. 77, fo. 40] for she was alive in Queen Marys & Queen Elizabeths time, as appears by her acquittances & other records of those dates, but she had no children by him. And she dyed among her freinds in Leicestershire, where she was buryed amongst her anncestors there.[25]

The Course of Life of this Henry Lord Clifford

This Henry Lord Clifford was born in 1454, the year after his grandfather Thomas Lord Clifford was slain, & this Henry was the first of the Lords Cliffords that was Baron Vesey,[26] which barony he had

[21] She was a daughter of Henry Pudsey of Bolton-by-Bolland and Barforth (*Dugdale's Visitation of Yorks.*, ed. J. W. Clay, ii. 274). Dugdale gives the date of her first marriage, to Thomas Talbot of Bashall, Craven, as 1505, but the Talbots' own pedigree puts it in 9 Henry VII, and says that Thomas died before 13 Henry VII (*Craven*, pedigree at p. 32).

[22] Dr. Williamson (*Lady Anne Clifford*, p. 18) saw at Lowther Castle a receipt dated 22 Henry VIII, in which Sir John Lowther acknowledged receiving from Richard, abbot of Shap, £50, in full payment of 300 marks owed to him by the first Earl of Cumberland in connection with the marriage between his son Hugh Lowther and the Earl's sister Dorothy Clifford. On their numerous offspring, see *Pedigrees . . . of Cumberland and Westmorland*, ed. J. Foster, p. 84.

[23] This marriage took place about 1524, when the Lady Florence received a portion from the Cliffords. Cf. G. C. Williamson, *op. cit.*, p. 17.

[24] I.e. the second Marquess (1477-1530), whose other three sons fell into catastrophe in 1554.

[25] I.e. with the Greys, whose houses were at Groby and at Bradgate near Leicester.

[26] G.E.C., iii. 294, remarks that the peerage of de Vescy had legally become extinct, having been expressly limited to heirs male by the writ of 24 January 1449, which originated it. Nevertheless, Lord Clifford and his heir are both recognised in the patent rolls as 'Lord Clifford Westmorland and Vescy.'

by inheritance from his mother, so as he was commonly stiled in patents & other writings by King Henry the 7th & Henry the 8th, Lord & Baron of Clifford, Westmoreland & Vesey & Lord of the honor of Skypton in Craven; & as it is said before, he could not exceed the age of 6 or 7 years old when his father John Lord Clifford was slain at the battle of Towton near Ferry bridge in Yorkshire, the 28th or 29th of March in 1461, the first year of Edward the 4th. This Henry Lord Clifford was one of the examples of the variety of fortunes in this world, for tho he was born the eldest son to a great nobleman, yet presently after his fathers death, when himself was about 7 years old, he was by the care & love of an industrious mother put into the habit of a shepherds boy to conceal his birth & parentage, for had he been known to have been his fathers son & heir, in all probability he would either have been put in prison, or bannished, or put to death, so odious was the memory of his father for killing the young Earl of Rutland, & for being such a desperate commander in battle against the house of York, which then reigned. So in the condition of a shepherds boy at Lonnesborrow[27] where his mother lived then for the most part, did this Lord Clifford spend his youth, till he was about 14 years of age, about which time his mothers father Henry Bromflett Lord Vesey deceased.[28]

And a little after his death, it came to be murmured at court that his daughters 2 sons were alive, about which their mother was examined, but her answers were that she had given directions to send them both beyond seas, to be bred there, & she did not know whether they were dead or alive, which equivocation of hers did the better pass, because [p. 78, fo. 40v] presently after her husbands death, she sent both her sons away to the sea side, the younger of which, called Richard Clifford, was indeed transported over the seas into the Low Countries to be bred there, where he dyed not long after: so as his elder brother Henry Lord Clifford had, after his restitution, the enjoyment of that little estate, that this Richard his younger brother should have had if he had lived, as appears by the records in Henry the 7th's time.

But her eldest son Henry Lord Clifford was secretly conveyed back to Lonnesborrow again, & committed in the hands of shepherds as aforesaid, which shepherds wives had formerly been servants in that family, as attending the nurse that gave him suck, which made him,

[27] Londesborough. Cf. *supra*, p. 19.

[28] Cf. *supra*, p. 129, n. 9.

being a child, more willing to submit to that mean condition, where they infused into him that belief, that he must either be content to live in that manner, or be utterly undone.

And as he did grow to more years, he was still more capable of his danger, if he had been discovered, & therefore presently after his grandfather the Lord Vesey was dead, the said rumor of his being alive, being more & more whispered at the court, made his said loving mother by the means of her 2d husband Sir Lancelot Thirkeld to send him away with the said shepherds & their wives into Cumberland, to be kept as a shepherd there, sometimes at Thrilcot,[29] & amongst his father in laws kindred, & sometimes upon the borders of Scotland, where they took land purposely for those shepherds who had the custody of him, where many times his father in law came purposely to visit him, & sometimes his mother, though very secretly. N.B.[30] By which mean kind of breeding this inconvenience befell him, that he could neither write nor read; for they durst not bring him up in any kind of learning, for fear least by it, his birth should be discovered, yet after he came to his lands & honors, he learned to write his name only. Notwithstanding which disadvantage, after he came to be restored again to the enjoyment of his fathers estate, he came to be a very wise man, & a very good mannager of his estate and fortunes.

And after this Henry Lord Clifford had lived 24 or 25 years in this obscure manner with shepherds, & that himself was grown to be about 31 or 32 years old, Henry the 7th then obtaining his crown, did in the 1st parliament of his reign in 1486 restore the said Henry Lord Clifford in his blood and honor & to all his baronies, castles & lands of inheritance both in Westmoreland, Craven & elsewhere in England. Which restoration was the chief ground of the Lady Anne Clifford, now Countess Dowager of Pembrook, her title to the lands of inheritance, which by Gods blessing she now injoys both in [p. 79, fo. 41] Westmoreland & in Craven.

This Henry Lord Clifford after he came to be possessor of his said

[29] Threlkeld, near Keswick. Sir Lancelot (d. 1512) was a substantial landowner with three houses, at Threlkeld, Yanwath and Crosby Ravensworth (D. Scott, *Bygone Cumberland and Westmorland*, p. 5). In Crosby Ravensworth church are his tomb and an arch of the chancel, rebuilt by him and showing his arms impaling Bromflete quartering Vescy (*Hist. Monuments Comm.*, *Westmorland*, pp. 79-80). On Yanwath Hall, see *ibid.*, p. 250, and on the traditional hiding-place of the Shepherd Lord there, G. C. Williamson, *Lady Anne Clifford*, p. 15.

[30] 'N.B.' a marginal addition in the same hand.

estate, was a great builder & repairer of all his castles in the North, which were much gone to decay when he came to enjoy them, for they had been in strangers hands about 24 or 25 years. Skypton Castle & the lands about it, had been given by King Edward the 4th to William Stanley, whose head was cut of, after, about the 10th year of King Henry the 7th; and Westmoreland was given by Edward the 4th to his brother Richard of Gloucester, who was afterwards King of England & slain in battle the 22d of August in 1485.[31]

This Henry Lord Clifford did, after he came to his estate, exceedingly delight in Astronomy, & the contemplation of the course of the stars, which it is likely he was seasoned in, during the time of his shepherds life. He built a great part of Barden Tower, which is now much decayed, & there he lived much, which it is thought he did the rather because in that place he had furnished himself with materials & instruments for that study.

He was a plain man & lived for the most part a countrey life, & came seldom either to the court or to London, but when he was called thither to sit in them as a peer of the realm, in which Parliament it is reported he behaved himself wisely & nobly like a good English man. About the 21st year of King Henry the 7th, he the said Lord Clifford was in some disgrace with the said King, so as the said King caused him to bring into the publick court, all his evidences to shew by what right he held his lands in Westmoreland, & the sheriffwick of that county, as appears by some records, which pleadings & records did much help forward to the manifestation of the title & right of the Lady Anne Clifford, now Countess Dowager of Pembrook, to the said lands & sheriffwick.[32]

This Henry Lord Clifford through the provident government of his estate, grew to be a very rich man, both in mony, chattells and goods, and great stocks of ground. But he was very unfortunate in having great unkindness between himself & his eldest son Henry Clifford for some 7 or 8 years before his death.

For that son of his, after his mother Anne St. John, Lady Clifford her death, and that his father was married again to a 2d wife, grew into great angers against his fathers wife, & his fathers servants, as appears by some letters,[33] which are still extant; which angers

[31] These grants actually appear in the patent rolls. Cf. *Y.A.J.*, xviii. 370-1.

[32] Cf. *supra*, p. 130, n. 11.

[33] Lady Anne had evidently seen other letters besides the one mentioned *supra*, p. 21, which does not, at all events as printed by Whitaker, mention the quarrel between the son and his step-mother.

between them was a great misfortune to them both, & to all that pertained unto them. It was also a misfortune to this Henry Lord Clifford that, some two years before his death, in the 13th year of King Henry the 8th in 1521, his ancient & great castle of Brough under Stainmore in Westmoreland was set on fire by a casual mischance, a little after he had kept a great Christmas there, so as all the timber & lead was utterly consumed, & nothing left but the bare [p. 80, fo. 41v] walls standing,[34] which since are more & more consumed & quite ruinated, for his son lived so much at the court that he had no time to repair it, and his grand child the 2d Earl of Cumberland bestowed so much in repairing Brougham Castle, as kept him from doing anything to Brough Castle; and George Earl of Cumberland spent so much in 9 or 10 sea voyages as that he repaired none of his castles, & so this Brough Castle went to utter ruin & decay more & more.

This Henry Lord Clifford, when he was about 69 or 70 years old and had lived possessor of his lands & honors 37 years & upwards, dyed the 23d of April in 1523, the 15th of Henry the 8th, as appears by the inquisitions.

And certainly he was buryed either in Shap Abby in Westmoreland or in Bolton Abby in Craven, for he dyed in the North & left directions in his will to bury him in one of those 2 Abbys if he dyed in the North.[35]

His eldest son Henry Lord Clifford was 30 years old and upwards when his said father dyed, as appears by inquisitions; and 2 years & 3 months after his fathers death he was created first Earl of Cumberland of that family of Cliffords, by King Henry the 8th in his Palace of Bridewell in London, the 18th of June 1525.

[p. 81, fo. 42]

A Summary of the Records of Henry Lord Clifford of Westmoreland and of the Honor of Skypton in Craven & Baron Vesey, who was the first of his family that was created Earl of Cumberland; he marryed

[34] Cf. *supra*, p. 77.

[35] Cf. *supra*, p. 21, n. 26. Richard Bank, the writer of the letter there mentioned, was probably at Hornby Castle (cf. *L. & P.*, iv.(1). 235) when he reported that young Lord Clifford had requested him to be at old Lord Clifford's burial. This does not help to decide between Shap and Bolton, but it shows that the interment took place nearly a year after Clifford's death. The date of the latter event, and also that of Lord Monteagle's death (cf. G.E.C., ix. 115), make it impossible to transfer Bank's letter from 1524 to 1523. Bank himself belonged to a notable Craven family. Cf. pedigree in *Craven*, at p. 236.

to his first wife Margaret Talbot, & to his 2d wife Margaret Peircy, by whom he had all his children.

This Henry Lord Clifford, afterwards first Earl of Cumberland, by computation was born in the year 1493, for he was about 30 years old when his father dyed, which was the 23d of Aprill in the year 1523. He was about 2 years & 2 months after his fathers death created first Earl of Cumberland of that family of the Cliffords by King Henry the 8th in his palace of Bridewell, the 18th day of June 1525, the 17th year of King Henry the 8th. He lived possessor of his lands & estate about 19 years, & Earl of Cumberland 17 years wanting 2 months, being about 23 years old, when his son Henry Lord Clifford was born, who was afterwards 2d Earl of Cumberland, which 2d Earl of Cumberland was 6 years old, when his grandfather Henry Lord Clifford dyed in 1523, as before.

This Henry Lord Clifford, first Earl of Cumberland, dyed the 22d of Aprill 1542 in the 34th year of King Henry the 8th, being then by computation about 49 years old, as appears by inquisitions. He dyed in Skypton Castle, and was buried in the vault in Skipton church in Craven.

His Wives

His first wife was Margaret Talbott, eldest daughter to George Talbott, 4th Earl of Shrewsbury, but she dyed very young, without children, within a year or two after marriage. And it is remarkable that this Lady Margaret Talbott her sister Elizabeth Talbott, was wife to William Lord Dacres of Gillesland & mother to that Anne Dacres that was many years after 2d wife to his eldest son Henry, after 2d Earl of Cumberland, & mother to George Earl of Cumberland, and the said Lady Margaret Talbott was buried in the vault in Skypton church.

His Second Wife

His second wife was the Lady Margaret Peircy, first child & only daughter to Henry Peircy first [*in right margin:* fifth?] Earl of Northumberland & sister to Henry the 6th Earl of Northumberland, who was called the Unthrifty Earl, & dyed without children. [p. 82, fo. 42v]. Which Lady Margaret Peircy had given her dowry by her father, and afterwards confirmed by her elder brother, all those lands in Craven called by the name of Peircy Fee, which elder brother of hers was called the Unthrifty Earl of Northumberland, & dyed without children, which made him the more willing to confirm the said lands called Peircy Fee to his said sister & her posteritie.

And this Lady Margaret, Countess of Cumberland, her mother that Countess of Northumberland was Catherine, daughter & one of the coheirs of Robert Spencer Kt. by Elianor his wife, daughter & at length coheir to Edmond Beufort, Duke of Somersett;[36] so as by her, this daughter of hers, Margaret Countess of Cumberland, was lineally descended from John of Gaunt Duke of Lancaster, & consequently from King Edward the 3d. And besides her great birth, she was a lady of great piety, virtue & goodness, & lived for the most part a country life in the North, tho her husband was much at the court.

She was born 10 or 11 years before any of her brothers, & lived so long only child to her father & mother, so as they resolved to give her a good portion in lands, tho she had a brother; which they performed by giving her the lands of Peircy's Fee. She had only 5 children by this Earl of Cumberland that lived any time, & she was happy in seeing her eldest son marryed to that great fortune, the Lady Ellianor Grace, daughter to Charles Brandon by the French Queen, & to see the said Lady Elianor to leave her first child by her eldest son, which first child was the Lady Margaret Clifford, long time after marryed to Henry Stanley Earl of Derby. And this Margaret Peircy, Countess of Cumberland, dyed widow to the said Earl her husband about 2 years after his death,[37] & was buryed by him in the vault of Skypton church in Craven.

Their Children

Henry Lord Clifford, their eldest son & heir, who succeeded his father in the Earldom of Cumberland and in his other lands and

[36] The fifth Earl of Northumberland married (before 1502) Katherine, daughter and coheir of Sir Robert Spencer of Spencercombe, Devon, by Eleanor, daughter (and in her issue coheir) of Edmund Beaufort, Duke of Somerset (d. 1455). The other daughter and coheir Margaret Spencer married Thomas Cary and was grandmother of the first Lord Hunsdon (G.E.C., ix. 720). Katherine's will is in *Test. Ebor.*, vi. 166-8; it was proved at York 9 November 1542.

[37] Actually she predeceased him, dying 25 November 1540, as shown by her Latin inscription at Skipton (*Craven*, p. 430).

honors, was born in the year 1517, and about 6 years before his grandfather Henry Lord Clifford dyed; which grandfather of his, as we have it by tradition, did believe by the skill he had in Astronomy that this young grandchild of his should beget 2 sons, between whose posterity there should be great suits in law, & that the heirs male of his line should end in those 2 sons, or presently after them.[38]

[p. 83, fo. 43]
This Henry, 2d Earl of Cumberland, dyed the 8th of January in Brougham Castle in Westmoreland in the year 1570, computing the year to begin on New Years day.

Ingram Clifford the 2d son marryed Anne, daughter & sole heir to Sir Henry Rowcliffe Kt.,[39] by whom he had great inheritance, & they had issue 2 daughters which both dyed before them; so he, dying without issue, left his nephew George Earl of Cumberland his heir in the year [*blank*].[40]

The Lady Katherine Clifford their first daughter was marryed first to John Lord Scroope of Bolton Castle in Yorkshire, and afterwards to Sir Richard Cholmondeley, & had issue by both her husbands, so as this Sir Hugh Cholmondely & Sir Henry Cholmondeley, brothers now living,[41] are the first in descent from this Lady Katherine Clifford by her 2d husband.

The Lady Maud Clifford was marryed to Sir John Coniers,[42] eldest son to the Lord Coniers of Horneby Castle in Yorkshire, by whom she had diverse children.[43]

The Lady Elizabeth Clifford was marryed to Sir Christopher Metcalfe Kt.,[44] by whom she had diverse children, from whom the Metcalfs & other familys of note there are descended.

[38] An allusion to the prolonged lawsuits between Lady Anne and her male relatives, and to the deaths of the fourth and fifth Earls in 1641-3.

[39] Of Cowthorpe, near Wetherby. Cf. *Glover's Visitation*, p. 285.

[40] For Sir Ingram Clifford's will (proved 6 July 1579), and the lands he inherited from Anne Rowcliffe and left to his nephews, see *Y.A.J.*, xviii. 380.

[41] A reference to Sir Hugh Cholmeley, the famous Royalist defender of Scarborough (1600-1657), and Sir Henry Cholmeley, the lawyer, of West Newton Grange (d. 1666). They were great-grandsons of Katherine Clifford (J. Foster, *Yorkshire Pedigrees*, iii).

[42] I.e. the third Lord Conyers. On this marriage see supra, p. , and nos. 24, 25. He died in 1557 without male heirs, the barony falling into abeyance between his daughters (G.E.C., iii. 405).

[43] Listed in Clay, p. 35.

[44] Of Nappa in Wensleydale, 1513-74. On this marriage (*c.* 1550) and their children see *Metcalfe Records*, pp. 99-101 and pedigree at p. 1.

The Lady Jane Clifford marryed to Sir John Huddlestone Kt.[45]

The Course of Life of this Henry Lord Clifford first Earl of Cumberland.

This Henry Lord Clifford, first Earl of Cumberland, was almost a perfect contemporary with King Henry the 8th, for he was born in the year 1493, two years after the said King was born, & dyed about 4 years & nine months before him. He was bred up for the most part, in his childhood and youth, with the said King, both when he was Duke of York, & when he was Prince, which ingrafted such a love in the said Prince towards him, that it continued even to the very end; which love between them was nourished the more because they were of kindred the one to the other, for King Henry the 7th was cousin german by the half blood to Anne St. John this Earles mother, who was a saintly and blessed woman.

But this Earl of Cumberland living so much about the court in his youth drew him so much to love London & the southern parts, as that there he became a great waster of his estate, which caused him after to sell much fair lands & possessions, & more than his ancestors had consumed in many years before.

[p. 84, fo. 43v] It also, as is thought, made him more stout & less submitting to his old father Henry Lord Clifford, than otherwise he would have been, for there was great dissentions betwixt him & his father, especially after his father was marryed to his 2d wife. He was, as appears by inquisition, 30 years old & upwards when his said father Henry Lord Clifford dyed about the 22d of April in 1523; and two years & 2 months after that, in the Palace of Bridewell in London, he was created Earl of Cumberland, the 18th day of June in 1525 in the 17th year of King Henry the 8th, by the said King.

The words of his patent make manifest declaration of the high esteem and great repute he was in with the said King, wherein the said patents & diverse other patents stiled him Baron Clifford, Westmoreland & Vesey. And the same day in the same place, was Thomas Manners, Lord Rosse created Earl of Rutland.[46]

[45] Of Millom, Cumberland. Cf. *Pedigrees . . . of Cumberland and Westmorland*, ed. J. Foster, p. 64. According to this pedigree, she was the first of his three wives.

[46] Cf. G.E.C., iii. 566; xi. 254; the ceremony is further described in Hall, *Chronicle*, edn. 1809, p. 703.

The said King also made the said Earl of Cumberland knight of the most noble Order of the Garter, the 28th or 29th year of his reign.[47] He made him also Lord President of the north parts of England,[48] & many times Lord Warden of the Marches of the west borders of Cumberland, over against Scotland, for this Lord was still imployed in all the armies which were sent out of England into Scotland, and behaved himself very nobly & valiantly in them.

Also the King permitted the said Earl to purchase of him the abby of Bolton in Craven & all the lands belonging to it, at a very easy and cheap rate, which lands are now in the possession of the Lady Elizabeth Clifford, now wife to Richard Boyle Earle of Corke.[49]

But the greatest favour wherein the said King did express the most of his affection & respect unto this Earl, was his willingness to have his niece, the Lady Elianor Brandon, his youngest sisters youngest daughter, marryed to this Earles eldest son, Henry Lord Clifford; which marriage was accomplished & solemnized at midsummer the 27th year of his reign in 1537 in the house of her father Charles Brandon Duke of Suffolk; which house was then a goodly palace in Southwark near London, & hard by St. Mary Overy's there, the King himself being present in person at the marriage; which marriage was solemnized that time 4 years after the death of the said Lady Elianors mother, who was Mary the French Queen.[50]

And for the more magnificent entertainment of this young lady, the Lady Elianors Grace, against her coming down to Skypton in Craven, her father in law caused the great gallery at Skypton & the tower at the east end thereof, being 8 square round,[51] with rooms underneath them both, to be all built from the ground, in 3 months space, & a way made out of the great castle itself into the said gallery; which building was erected for the greater honor of that castle &

---

[47] He was instituted to the order 13 May 1537 (*ibid.*, iii. 567).

[48] Dr. Reid's researches did not reveal any commission to Cumberland as President, but he was a member of the Council in the North from January 1537 to his death. Cf. *supra*, p. 25.

[49] Elizabeth, daughter of Henry Clifford, fifth Earl of Cumberland, married (3 July 1634) Richard Boyle, Viscount Dungarvan, later second Earl of Cork and first Earl of Burlington (d. 1697; she d. 1691). On Lady Anne's death in 1676, a division of the Clifford estates brought the Bolton and Londesborough lands to this pair, and so to the Earls of Cork (*ibid.*, iii. 302; Clay, p. 16).

[50] Mary died 25 June 1533 (G.E.C., xii(1). 459); her daughter's marriage to Clifford actually took place in 1535, not 1537. Cf. *infra*, p. 144, n. 57.

[51] I.e. octagonal, as may be observed. This domestic portion of the castle was spared in the slighting of 1649, to which Lady Anne refers *infra*.

delight to the said young lady against her coming down thither, where she was entertained within 4 or 5 months after her marriage by her father in law & the Countess his wife, with all the respect, love and reverence that might be; and both lived to see this young lady have children, [p. 85, fo. 44] though all her issue male dyed in their infancy and none of her children lived to any years, but the Lady Margaret, she that was afterwards Countess of Derby.

Which gallery & tower so suddenly built is now the chief mansion house to the Lady Anne Clifford, Countess of Pembrook, when she resided [*sic*] in Craven, & the round tower there is the said Countess her lodgeing chamber, the castle itself being totally demolished in December 1649[52] and in the month following, by reason of those late unhappy differences and civil wars in England, having been made a garrison on both sides.

This Earl of Cumberland was one of the most eminent lords of his time, for nobleness, gallantry & courtship.

This Henry Clifford, first Earl of Cumberland, dyed in the castle of Skypton in Craven the 22d of April 1542, the 34th year of Henry the 8th, he being then about 49 years old at the time of his death. And his dead body was buried in the vault at Skypton church in Craven, & his wife Margaret Peircy Countess of Cumberland dyed about 2 years after,[53] and was buried in the same vault hard by him.

This first Earl of Cumberland lived possessor of his lands & ancient honors after his fathers death 19 years, and Earl of Cumberland 17 years, wanting two months, his eldest son Henry Lord Clifford being then 23 ['23' *cancelled and* '25' *substituted in right margin*] years old & upwards,[54] as appears by the inquisitions taken after his said fathers death.

[p. 86, fo. 44v]

A summary of the Records concerning Henry Lord & Baron Clifford, Westmoreland & Vesey, & Lord of the Honor of Skypton, & 2d Earl of Cumberland, who marryed to his first wife the Lady's Grace,

[52] On the preceding sieges, cf. *Craven*, pp. 412 *seqq.*

[53] Cf. *supra*, p. 138, n. 37.

[54] He was born 1517 and on the death of his father in 1542 was thus about 25 years of age.

Elianor Brandon, & to his 2d wife Anne Dacres, he being the 16th Lord Baron & High Sheriff of Westmoreland and 13th Lord of the Honor of Skypton in Craven.

This Henry Lord Clifford, second Earl of Cumberland, was by computation born in the year 1517, for he is set down to be 25 years old & more at his father's death, which was the 22d of April in 1542, as appears by the inquisitions. And it is evident he was about 6 years old, at the death of his grandfather Henry Lord Clifford, whom we call the Shepherd, because he lived so long amongst Shepherds.

This Henry Lord Clifford, 2d Earl of Cumberland, dyed in Brougham Castle in Westmoreland the 8th day of January 1570, computing the year at New Years Day, as appears by the inquisitions after his death. So by computation he was about 48 [48 *cancelled and* 41 *substituted in left margin*] years old, when his son George Lord Clifford, who was afterwards 3d Earl of Cumberland, was born into the world at Brougham Castle in Westmoreland, and by the same account he must needs be 53 years old, when he the said 2d Earl of Cumberland died.

And though he dyed at Brougham Castle, as aforesaid, yet his dead body was buryed in the vault at Skypton church in Craven. This Henry Lord Clifford lived 2d Earl of Cumberland 28 years, wanting some 3 months and 14 days, at which time his then eldest son George Lord Clifford was 14 [14 *cancelled and* 11 *substituted in left margin*] years old[55] & 5 months and succeeded his father in his lands & honors.

His First Wife

His first wife was the Lady's Eleanor Brandon Grace,[56] who was youngest daughter to Charles Brandon Duke of Suffolk, by his wife Mary, the French Queen. And he was marryed to the said Lady Elianor when he was between 19 & 20 years old, being then but Lord

[55] He was born 8 August 1558 and was 11 years 5 months old on his accession. Cf. G. C. Williamson, *George, Third Earl of Cumberland*, p. 2.

[56] 'Grace' first written after 'Lady's'; then cancelled and interpolated after 'Brandon'.

Clifford, about Midsummer the 27th year of Henry the 8th, in the year of Our Lord 1537.[57]

And they were married together in her father the Duke of Suffolks palace or house in Southwark near St Mary Overys near London Bridge. In which church of St. Mary Overys just that time 40 years after[58] was George Clifford Earl of Cumberland marryed to the Lady Margaret Russell his wife, in Southwark aforesaid. This Lady Elianor her mother Mary the French Queen dyed [p. 87, fo. 45] just 4 years after[59] she was marryed to this Henry Lord Clifford. And this Lady Elianor [Grace *interpolated*] lived wife to the said Lord some 10 years and 5 months, & dyed in Brougham Castle in Westmoreland, about the latter end of November in 1547, the first year of King Edward the 6th, after she had lived Countess of Cumberland 5 years, 7 months & 10 days or thereabouts. Her dead body was buryed in the vault in the parish of Skypton in Craven, where her said husband was afterwards buried. And it is believed she was not above 27 or 28 years of age at the time of her death.

This high-born Princess Elianor, Countess of Cumberland, was grandchild to King Henry the 7th, niece to King Henry the 8th & cousin german to King Edward the 6th, Queen Mary, & Queen Elizabeth, & to King James the 5th, King of Scotland. She was also cosin german twice removed to the Earl of Cumberland her husband, by the blood of the St. Johns.[60]

His Children by his First Wife

First the Lady Margaret Clifford, who was born in Brougham Castle in Westmoreland in the year 1540, when her father in law,[61] viz. her husbands father, was living, & when she[62] came to be about 7 years old, her said mother dyed. This Lady Margaret, when she was about 15 years old, was marryed in much glory in the chappel at Whitehall, King Philip & Queen Mary being both present at the said marriage, to Henry Stanley Lord Strange, on the 7th day of

[57] The year 1537 is a slip: 27 Henry VIII began on 22 April 1535, which was the actual year of the marriage. The Act concerning Eleanor's jointure was passed on 4 February 1536 (*L. & P.*, x. 243(8)).

[58] On 24 June 1577 (*Lives of Lady Anne Clifford*, p. 3).

[59] For ' before ', but even this is in error. Cf. *supra*, p. 141, n. 50.

[60] Cf. *supra*, p. 129.

[61] I.e. Eleanor's father-in-law, the first Earl.

[62] I.e. Margaret Clifford.

February in the year 1555.[63] Which said Lord Strange by the death of his father Edward Earl of Derby, on the 4th of October 1572.[64] This said Henry Earl of Derby was afterwards made Knight of the Garter, & dyed in the year 1593.

And his wife, the said Margaret Clifford Countess of Derby, overlived him three years and more, for she dyed the 29th of September in the year 1596, in her house then newly built in Clerkenwell, without the Close at London, when she was about 56 years old, & was buryed in the Abby at Westminster. She had two sons by him, Ferdinando & William, who were successively, one after another, Earls of Derby. Her eldest son Ferdinando Earl of Derby dyed before her, leaving no children but daughters behind him, the 16th of April 1594. Her second son William Earl of Derby dyed a little before Michaelmas [p. 88, fo. 45v] in the year 1641, leaving his son James Earl of Derby to succeed him, who was beheaded at Bol[ton] in Lancaster[65] in October 1651.

The 2d child of this Lady Elianors Grace by her husband, Henry Earl of Cumberland, was Henry Lord Clifford, who dyed in his infancy, when he was but 2 or 3 years old, & was buryed [in] the vault at Skypton church in Craven. Charles Clifford, their 2d son & 3d child, dyed also in his infancy, & was buryed in the place aforesaid.

So this Lady Elianors Grace left no children behind her, but only the Lady Margaret Clifford, afterwards Countess of Derby.

His Second Wife Anne Dacres

His 2d wife was Anne Dacres, youngest daughter to William Lord Dacres of Gillesland & Graystock in Cumberland, by his wife the Lady Elizabeth Talbott, daughter to George Talbott Earl of Shrewsbury.

Which Elizabeth was eldest sister to that Margaret who was first wife to Henry Clifford first Earl of Cumberland, but she dyed very young before she had any child.

This Anne Dacres was marryed in her fathers house called

[63] On the previous abortive plan to marry Margaret to Sir Andrew Dudley, see G. C. Williamson, *Lady Anne Clifford*, pp. 23-4.

[64] *Sic*, presumably intending to record his succession to the Earldom. The correct date is 24 October 1572 (G.E.C., iv. 210-11).

[65] Bolton, Lancashire, where the Earl was beheaded, after a court martial of the Parliamentary army, 15 October 1651 (*ibid.*, iv. 214-15).

Kirkouswald Castle in Cumberland to Henry 2d Earl of Cumberland, about the latter end of King Edward the 6ths time, in the year 1552, or 1553.[66] Which Earl made to the said Lady Anne his wife in joynture, during her life, all his lands in Westmoreland was [*sic*] confirmed to her under the Great Seal of England by King Philip & Queen Mary, for the more surety of it, because it was crown lands.

This Lady Anne Dacres Countess of Cumberland lived this Earles wife about 17 or 18 years, & his widow about 11 years & 6 months, for she dyed in Skypton Castle about the latter end of July in 1581 & was buryed in the vault of the church of Skypton by her husband & his first wife, her son George Earl of Cumberland & his wife being present with her at her death.

She was by computation about 48 years old when she dyed, her eldest son George Earl of Cumberland being then near 23 years old: and remarkable it is in this Anne Countess of Cumberlands life, that she never was at London, nor near it, but applyed herself in domestick & home affairs, while she was maid, wife & widow. [p. 89, fo. 46]

His Children by his Second Wife

Their first child was the Lady Frances Clifford, born in Skypton Castle 1555. She was marryed to Philip Lord Wharton, at the same time & in the same place, that her brother George Earl of Cumberland was marryed to the Lady Margaret Russell.[67] This Lady Frances Clifford had by her husband divers children, wherof her eldest son Sir George Wharton was slaine at a private quarrel at Islington near London in November 1609,[68] and her 2d son Sir Thomas Wharton, who dyed that day 30 years after her, who was father to Philip, now Lord Wharton[69] & to his brother Sir Thomas Wharton.

This Ladys first child was Margaret Wharton, who is, and hath been long, widdow to Edward Lord Wotton, a worthy lady,[70] and this Lady Frances Clifford, wife to Philip Lord Wharton, dyed in her husbands house called Wharton Hall in Westmoreland the 16th

[66] I observe no precise date elsewhere.

[67] Cf. *supra*, p. 144.

[68] He and his antagonist, Sir James Stewart, Master of Blantyre, were both slain, 8 November 1609. Cf. references in G.E.C., xii(2). 601-2.

[69] The famous Parliamentarian and Whig peer (1613-1696).

[70] Lord Wotton d. 1625 (G.E.C., xii(2). 867); his wife Margaret d. 10 March 1659 (*Lives of Lady Anne Clifford*, p. 90). She was a prominent Roman Catholic.

of April in 1592, and was buryed in the church of Kirkby Stephen there in the said county, when she was about 37 years old,[71] where her youngest child Frances, wife to Sir Richard Musgrave, was buryed many years after.[72]

The Lady Mary Clifford, second child to this Earl of Cumberland by his 2d wife, was born in Skypton Castle 1556 & dyed when she was about 2 or 3 years old, & was buryed in Appleby church in Westmorland.

Their 3d child was Elianor Clifford, born also in Skypton Castle 1557, & she dyed a maid when she was about 14 or 15 years old, & was buried in Appleby church in Westmoreland, her mother being then a widow.

Their 4th child & first son, was George Lord Clifford, who was after Earl of Cumberland. He was born in Brougham Castle in Westmoreland the 8th of August in 1558, about 3 months and 10 days before the death of Queen Mary, so as he was just 11 years & five months old at the death of his father, who dyed about the 8th of January in 1570, as the year begins on New Years Day; so as this Earl George lived a ward to Queen Elizabeth 10 years & odd months. He was the 3d Earl of Cumberland of his family, & last heir male of the Cliffords that was rightfully possessed of their antient lands & honors in Craven & Westmoreland. He dyed at the Duchy House at the Savoy by London the 30th day of October in 1605, when he was 47 years old, 2 months & 22 days over. His dead body was buryed in the vault of the church of Skypton in Craven the 13 day of March following. [p. 90, fo. 46v] He left only one legitimate child behind him, who was his daughter & sole heir, the Lady Anne Clifford, after Countess of Dorsett, & now Countess Dowager of Pembrooke & Montgomery.

Their 5th child & 2d son, Francis Clifford, who was born in Skypton Castle the 30th of October in 1559 in the 1st year of Queen Elizabeth; & by reason his elder brother George dyed without heirs male, he came to be the 4th Earl of Cumberland the same day that himself was 46 years old; which Earldom he enjoyed 35 years & 3 months, wanting 10 days, so as by computation he was 82 years & 3 months old, wanting 10 days, when he dyed in Skypton Castle the 21st

[71] Lady Frances appears, with an inscription by Lady Anne, in the two great family portraits of the Cliffords. Cf. *Craven*, pp. 339, 343; G. C. Williamson, *Lady Anne Clifford*, pp. 339-40.

[72] Frances married Sir Richard Musgrave of Edenhall, who became a baronet in 1611. Cf. *Pedigrees . . . of Cumberland and Westmorland*, ed. J. Foster, p. 93.

of January in 1641, as the year begins on New Years Day.[73] And his dead body was buryed in the vault of Skypton church in Craven. And his only son Henry Clifford Earl of Cumberland dyed 2 years 10 months & 21 days after him in the city York, the 11th day of December in 1643, without issue male.[74]

The Course of Life of this Henry Lord Clifford, Second Earl of Cumberland

This Henry 2d Earl of Cumberland was born in the year of Our Lord 1517, about 6 years before the death of his grandfather Henry Lord Clifford. And when himself was about 16 years of age, he was made Knight of the Bath at the coronation of Queen Anne of Boleyn in 1533; and about 4 years after, when he was about 20 years old, he was marryed to the Lady Elianor Brandon her Grace [*the MS here repeats details of the marriage and their children, almost verbatim and without additions*]

[p. 91, fo. 47] This Lord, whom we now treat of, was never any ward, for he was 25 years and upwards, when his father Henry Clifford first Earl of Cumberland dyed, as appears by diverse inquisitions. He lived a widdower about 4 or 5 years after the death of his first wife, the Lady Elianors Grace, Countess of Cumberland, & when that time was expired, he marryed for his 2d wife Anne Dacres, by whom he had 2 sons, George & Francis, who were both Earls of Cumberland, & other children, as appears before.

This Henry 2d Earl of Cumberland was in his youth, before he betook himself to a retired country life, a great waster of his estate & sold much land; and amongst the rest he sold that remarkable mannor of Temedsbury or Tenbury, part whereof are [*sic*] in Worcestershire, & part in Herefordshire, which mannor was given in Henry the 3ds time by Walter Clifford 2d Lord Clifford of Clifford Castle in Herefordshire & his wife Agnes de Condy to their younger son Roger de Clifford & his wife Sybill de Ewias & their heirs, & was after confirmed to them by Maud de Longspee, daughter & sole heir to the said Walter Lord Clifford his eldest son, which mannor of Temedsbury did descend from the said Roger, on whom it was first conferred, unto his only son Roger de Clifford, who married Isabella

[73] Cf. *Lives of Lady Anne Clifford*, p. 50.

[74] He d. of a fever, on the date given, at one of the prebendal houses in York (*ibid.*, p. 52; G.E.C., iii. 570).

de Veteripont & so continued in the heirs male of the family of the Cliffords, descended from them for the space of 226 [*in right margin corrected to* 326] years, or thereabouts, when the said Henry Earl of Cumberland sold the same.[75] But after, towards his latter times, when the said Earl lived a country life, he grew so rich, as that he did purchase lands & leases & tythes to a great value, both of old Sir Thomas Chaloner,[76] the widow Lady Drury, & others.

He was about 30 years old when his first wife dyed, & he survived her 23 years & 40 days. And presently after her death he fell into an extream sickness, of which he was at length laid out for a dead man, upon a table, & covered with a hearse of velvet; but some of his men that were then very carefull about him perceiveing some little signs of life in him, did apply hot cordials inwardly & outwardly unto him, which brought him to life again, & so, after he was laid into his bed again, he was fain for 4 or 5 weeks after to suck the milk out of a woman's breast and only to live on that food; and after to drink asses milk, and live on that for 3 or 4 months longer. Yet after that, before the year [p. 92, fo. 47v] was ended, he became a strong able man, and so continued to be till a little before his death.

He was much addicted to the study and practice of Alchimy and Chimistry, & a great distiller of waters & making of other chimical extractions for medicines, & very studious in all manner of learning, so as he had an excellent library, both of written hand books and printed books. To which he was exceedingly addicted, especially towards his latter end, when he had given over living at the court & at London, to which places he came seldom after the death of his first wife; &, as we have heard, but 3 times, the first at the beginning of Queen Mary's reign to her coronation; the 2d time to his daughter the Lady Margaret Clifford's marriage with the Lord Strange, who was after Earl of Derby, when she was marryed to him in the year 1555, the 7th of February; and the 3d & last time he came up to London, was to see Queen Elizabeth & to present his duty to her, a little after she first came to be Queen.

He lived Earl of Cumberland about 28 years, wanting some 3 months & 14 days, & he dyed when he was about 53 years old. He departed this life in his castle of Brougham in Westmoreland the

[75] On Tenbury cf. *supra*, p. 26, n. 64; on these early Cliffords cf. *Y.A.J.* xviii. 354-6.

[76] Sir Thomas Challoner (1521-65) of Guisborough and of Steeple Claydon, Buckinghamshire; Councillor in the North, 1553-7 (*D.N.B.*; Reid, p. 493). He is called ' old to distinguish him from his son and namesake (1561-1615).

8th day of January in 1570, as the year begins on New Years Day, his 2d wife & all the children he had by her being then there with him, excepting his eldest son George Lord Clifford, who then lived in the house called Battaile in Sussex, which formerly was an abby, with his mothers sister & her husband, the then Lord Viscount Monntague.[77]

Which George Lord Clifford was then about 11 years & 5 months old, when he then came to be 3d Earl of Cumberland by the death of his said father, who dyed in the same house & chambre wherein his son George was born into the world.

This Henry Clifford 2d Earl of Cumberland was buried in the vault in Skypton church in Craven hard by his first wife and many of his ancestors.

[From this point, the MS is printed in *Lives of Lady Anne Clifford* (*Roxburghe Club*, 1916), pp. 1 *seqq*.]

[77] Anthony Browne, first Viscount Montague (*c.* 1528-92) of Battle Abbey and Cowdray Park, Sussex. His second wife was Magdalen, daughter of William, third Lord Dacre (G.E.C., ix. 97-9).

INDEX

Abergavenny (Burguynye), Lord, 82-3
Acworth, Thomas, 32, 37-8, 75-7
Aire Valley, 26
Airton (Areton), 131
Alanbridge, John, see Ledes
Alexander III of Scotland, 89
Alnwick, 108
Althorp, 16
Ancrum Moor, 122
Androwe, Thomas, 85
Appleby (Appilby), Anthony, 84
Appleby, 30, 92, 97; Castle, 16, 20, 21n., 81, 125, 127; church, 147
Arundel, Sir Thomas, 44-5
Aske, Christopher, 24, 51-2; Robert, 52, 122
Aysgarth, 50

Babthorpe, Sir William, 33-4, 102-3, 119-21
Bagot, Richard, abbot of Shap, 77-8
Bainbridge, Cardinal, 39, 91
Banbrige, see Baynbrigg
Bank, Richard, 136n.
Banks, Alexander, abbot of Furness, 59
Barden Tower, 19, 29, 55, 70, 85, 135
Barforth, 21, 113-14, 132n.
Barnard Castle, 51, 112-13
Barton, John, see Bretton
Bashall, 21, 132n.
Battle, Sussex, 150
Baudewynne, John, 85
Baynbrigg (Banbrige), family of, 64; Alan, 64-5, 71-2
Beareparke, Henry, 114
Beaufort, Edmund, Duke of Somerset, 138; Lady Eleanor, see Spencer
Bedale, 43-4
Bedfordshire, 20
Belbie, John, 73
Bell, Richard, Bishop of Carlisle, 39
Bensted, Edward, 97
Berie, William, 60-61
Berwick, Richard, 68
Berwick, Treaty of, 41; Castle, 131; Governor of, 20, 130-31
Beswick, 63, 65
Bethell, Sir Hugh, 113; Mr., 113-14
Beverley, 63, 65, 122
Bielby, 41n.
Bilbrough, 70; see Norton
Bishopdale, 119
Blackheath, 82-3
Bleatarn, 31, 57
Blenkinsop, Thomas, 51n.
Bletsoe, 20
Blyth, Nottinghamshire, 54
Boleyn, Queen Anne, 45, 47-8, 110, 148
Bolton Castle, 49, 50-52, 111-12, 115, 120-21
Bolton Hall, 50n.
Bolton Priory, 16, 20-21, 24, 26, 32, 42, 52-3, 85-6, 129, 136, 141
Bolton-by-Bolland, 21, 132n.
Bolton, Lancashire, 145
Bolton, Westmorland, 31, 78-9
Bonvisi, Antonio, 45
Borders, see Marches
Boroughbridge, 102
Borrowdale, 123
Bowes, family of, 131; George, 51, 112; Lady Joan, *née* Clifford, 131; Sir Ralph, 131; Sir Robert, 34, 50, 119-20, 122-3
Boyle, Elizabeth, Countess of Cork, 141; Richard, Viscount Dungarvan, later second Earl of Cork, 141n.
Bradgate, 132n.
Bradley, Craven, 26, 90
Brandon, Charles, Duke of Suffolk, 20n., 24, 26, 102, 104, 138, 141, 143-4; Lady Eleanor, see Clifford
Bretton (Barton), John, 122-3
Bridlington Priory, 20
Bristol (Bristow), 103
Broke, Sir Robert, 102-3

Bromflete, see Vescy
Brough, Westmorland, 31, 51, 77; Castle, 77, 136
Brougham Castle, 23n., 88, 136, 139, 143-4, 147, 149
Broughton, near Skipton, 60
Brown(e), Sir Anthony, 130; Anthony, 131; Anthony, first Viscount Montague (Montacute), 131, 150; Hugh, 60; Lucy, see Clifford; Lady Magdalen, *née* Dacre, 150n.
Burbanke, Thomas, 39; William, 29, 39-41, 82-4, 88, 89
Burgh, Thomas, 85
Byland Abbey (Beghland), 31, 57-8; abbot of, see Ledes

CALAIS, 83
Cambridge, 35, 37, 39, 40, 67, 69
Campeggio, Cardinal, 29, 41, 82-3
Campsall, 102
Canterbury, 83; Archbishop of, see Warham
Carleton, near Penrith, 89
Carlisle, 22n., 23, 27, 39, 48, 89, 99-100; archdeaconry of, 39-40; Bishops of, see Bell, Kite; priory of, 58-9; prior of, see Salkeld
Carlton, Craven, 26, 29, 90, 91, 125-6
Carlton Hall, 91
Carnaby, Sir Reynold, 45
Carr, Sir John, 22, 90
Carus, Thomas, 102-3
Cary, Thomas, 138n.
Castle Howard, 100
Cavendish, George, 45n., 105, 106
Cawood, 91
Cayton, 73
Challoner, Robert, 34, 119-21; Sir Thomas, the elder, 149; the younger, 149n.
Chamberlayn, Sir Edward, 106
Chapuys, Eustache, 110
Charles V, Emperor, 40, 107
Chatsworth, 16
Chester, County Palatine of, 103
Chichester, Bishop of, 82-3
Cholmeley (Cholmondeley), Francis, 52, 113-14; Henry, 52, 114; Sir Henry, 139; Sir Hugh, 139; Katherine, 113; Lady Katherine, see Scrope; Margaret, 113; Sir Richard, 52, 113, 139
Cleveland, 53
Clifford, Lady Anne, *née* St. John, 20, 128-30, 135, 140; Lady Anne, *née* Rowcliffe, 139; Anne, Countess of Cumberland, *née* Dacre, 27, 137, 143, 145-6; Lady Anne, Countess of Pembroke, &c., 17, 18, 19, 21n., 26-7, 53, 55n., 77, 126-8, 134-5, 142, 147; Charles, son of the second Earl, 145; Lady Dorothy, see Lowther; Eleanor, Countess of Cumberland, *née* Brandon, 17, 20n., 24, 26-7, 52, 54, 125-6, 138, 141-4, 148; Lady Eleanor, 147; Lady Elizabeth, see Metcalfe; Lady Elizabeth, see Bowes; Lady Florence, *née* Pudsey, 21, 113, 128, 131-2, 135-6, 140; Lady Frances, see Wharton; Francis, fourth Earl of Cumberland, 139n., 147-8; George, third Earl of Cumberland, 15, 28, 52, 113-14, 127, 136-7, 143-4, 146-8, 150; Henry, tenth Lord (the 'Shepherd Lord'), 15, 18-22, 28-30, 36-7, 39, 42, 53-5, 63-72, 82-5, 87, 90-92, 96-9, 113, 127-37, 139-40, 143, 148; Henry, first Earl of Cumberland, 15, 20-26, 30-34, 37, 39, 44, 46-8, 50-55, 57-62, 72-81, 85-7, 89-90, 93-6, 100-112, 114-25, 127, 130, 132n., 135-42, 148; Henry, second Earl of Cumberland, 15, 20, 26-8, 33, 54, 91, 117, 125-6, 137-9, 141-50; Henry, Lord Clifford, son of the second Earl, 145; Henry, fifth Earl of Cumberland, 128, 139n., 148; Sir Ingram, 139; Isabella, *née* Veteripont, 148-9; Lady Jane, see Huddlestone; Lady Joan, *née* Dacre, 97; John, ninth Lord, 18, 128, 132-3; Lady Katherine, see Scrope; Lady Lucy, *née* Brown, 130; Lady Mabel, see Fitzwilliam; Lady Margaret, *née* Bromflete (Vescy), later Threlkeld, 18, 19, 67, 84, 132-3; Lady Margaret, *née* Talbot, 23, 137, 145; Margaret, Countess of Cumberland, *née* Percy, 23, 25-6, 108-9, 137-8, 142; Lady Margaret, see Stanley; Margaret, Countess of Cumberland, *née* Russell, 113, 127, 144, 146; Lady Mary, 147; Lady Maud, see Conyers; Richard, 133; Robert, first Lord, 18; Roger de, the elder and the younger, 148; Thomas, eighth Lord, 97, 128, 132; Sir Thomas, 20, 22n., 89, 130-31; Walter, second Lord, 148

Clifford Castle, Herefordshire, 148
Clifton, family of, 54n.; Anne, *née* Clifford, 17, 54, 93-4, 131; Dorothy, 54n., Dr. Gamaliel, 93-4; Gervase, the elder, 93; the younger, 54; Robert, 54, 93, 131n.
Clifton, Nottinghamshire, 54, 93-4
Clifton, Westmorland, 116
Cockermouth Castle, 46, 104; honor of, 104
Colonna, family of, 47, 105; Cardinal of, 107
Conishead Priory, 39
Conyers, family of, 17; Lady Anne, 53-4, 95-6; Christopher, second Lord, 53-4, 95-6; John, third Lord, 53-4, 95-6, 139; John, *alias* Norton, 122-3; Lady Maud, *née* Clifford, 52n., 53, 95-6, 139
Copendale (Coppyndale), Edmund, 50, 122-3
Corby, Cumberland, 97
Cork, Earls of, see Boyle
Cottingham, East Yorkshire, 113
Coverham Abbey, 50
Cowdray House, Sussex, 131
Cowthorpe, 139n.
Craven, 16, 20, 22, 25-7, 128-9, 132n., 134, 136, 138, 142, 147
Creyke (Crake), Ralph, 113-14
Cromwell, Thomas, 24-5, 32-3, 38, 42, 44, 53, 60, 68, 79-80, 96, 100, 109-10, 119
Crosby Ravensworth, 134n.
Cumberland, 18, 19, 23, 24, 27n., 31-2, 45, 58, 89, 97, 129, 140n., 141, 146; Earls of, see Clifford
Cundall, Henry, abbot of Roche, 37, 75-7
Cundy (Condy), Agnes de, 148

DACRE OF GILSLAND, family of, 17, 22-4, 27, 30, 32-3, 47-8, 78-9, 100, 108; Anne, see Clifford; Sir Christopher, 31, 78-9, 89, 101; Lady Elizabeth, *née* Talbot, 137, 145; Joan, see Clifford; Leonard, 27; Mabel, see Scrope; Magdalen, see Browne; Thomas, second Lord, 22-3, 30, 32, 48, 50n., 53, 73, 96-9; William, third Lord, 23, 27, 31, 33, 48-9, 61, 78-9, 89, 99-101, 103, 105-6, 109, 137, 145, 150
Dale, Jane, 91; John, 29-30, 90-92
Dalton, Mr., 113-14
Danby, Sir Christopher, 51, 112; Lady Elizabeth, 112
Darcy, Sir George, 22; Thomas, Lord, 22, 25
Dauphin of France, 82
Dawson, Richard, 91-2
Derby, Earls of, see Stanley
Derbyshire, 22
Devonshire, Duke of, 16
Doncaster, 75
Dover, 82-3
Downholme, 111
Drury, Lady, 149
Dudley, Sir Andrew, 145n.
Durham, 122; County Palatine of, 27n.; Bishops of, 82-3; see Tunstall
Dutton, Richard, 52, 113-14
Dyer, Sir James, 102-3

EASBY ABBEY, 50
Eccleston, Henry, prior of Mountgrace, 36n.
Edenhall, 101, 147n.
Edward III, 116, 138; Edward IV, 19, 20, 128, 133, 135; Edward VI, 58, 102, 144, 146
Egglestone Abbey, 79
Elizabeth I, Queen, 27, 113, 132, 144, 147, 149
Ellerton, East Yorkshire, 113
Erasmus, 39-40
Eure (Evers), family of, 33; Sir Ralph, 122-3
Ewias, Sybil de, 148
Exley, Edward, 62-3, 68-9
Eynns, Thomas, 102-3

FAIRFAX, Nicholas, 101, 103; Sir William, 33, 113-14
Farnham, 131n.
Fenton, prebend of, 39
Ferrand, Christopher, 91; William, 91
Ferriby, North, 32, 42, 85-6
Ferrybridge, 133
Firth, see Methley
Fisher, Henry, 127; John, Bishop of Rochester, 24, 37, 67, 69
Fitzherbert (Fegharbard), Sir Anthony, 36, 70-73
Fitzwilliam, Lady Mabel, *née* Clifford, 131; William, Earl of Southampton, 119, 131
Flodden, 19, 49
Fountains Abbey, 33, 115; abbot of, 75
Fox, Richard, Bishop of Winchester, 82-3

Francis I of France, 82
Frear, Ralph, 31, 78
Freer House, 64
Frobisher, Thomas, see Normanton
Fulthorpe, family of, 64; Christopher, 64-3
Fulthorpe, 64
Furness Abbey, 30-31, 59-61, 123-4; abbots of, see Banks; Pele

Gardiner, Stephen, Bishop of Winchester, 40
Gargrave, 60
Garter King of Arms, 23
Gascoigne, Sir William, 68-9, 120-21; William, 120
Gawthorpe, 68, 120
Gaunt, John, Duke of Lancaster, 138
Giggleswick, 25
Gigli, Silvester de, Bishop of Worcester, 39
Gilling, near Helmsley, 60; near Richmond, 122
Goodrich, Richard, 102-3
Gosnall, Mr., 103
Grande Chartreuse, 28, 68-9
Grey, Anne, Lady Powys, 126; Edward, third Lord Powys, 126; Lord John, 102-3; Lord Richard, 132; Thomas, Marquess of Dorset, 132
Greystoke, family of, 100; Elizabeth, 23n., 48
Greystoke, 29, 39, 88, 145
Grice, Thomas, 72
Grindal, Archbishop Edmund, 116
Groby, 132n.
Grove, Nottinghamshire, 106
Guisborough (Gisborne), 149n.; Priory, 130
Gyllotson, John, 92
Gylpyng, Gyfflot, 123

Hackney, 110
Hall, Edward, 18
Hanworth, Middlesex, 22
Harlsey Castle, 73
Hart, 27n.
Hayton, 41n.
Helbeck Hall, 51, 112
Henry II, 57; Henry III, 89, 148; Henry VII, 20, 90, 128-30, 133-5, 144; Henry VIII, 15, 19, 21-3, 25-6, 30, 39, 40, 42, 45, 47, 53, 82-3, 87, 90, 93, 96-9, 105-11, 129-31, 133, 136-7, 140-42, 144
Hercy, Mr. and Mrs., 106-7
Hereford, 93; dean of, 93; Herefordshire, 148
Hexham, 110
Heywood, Thomas, 106
Higdon, Brian, dean of York, 29, 32 41-4, 84-6; John, 41
Hilton, Alexander, Lord, 64; Sir William ('Baron Hilton'), 64-5
Hilton, Durham, 64
Hinderskelfe Castle, 100-101
Hipswell, 64
Hodsock, 54, 93
Holgate, Robert, Bishop of Llandaff, later Archbishop of York, 25, 34, 119-20
Holm Cultram Abbey, 31, 61-2; abbot of, see Ireby
Hornby, 53; Castle, 136n., 139
Howard, Thomas, Earl of Surrey and second Duke of Norfolk, 19, 82-3; Thomas, third Duke of Norfolk, 24-5, 44, 47, 105, 110
Hudleston, Lady Jane, *née* Clifford, 52n., 140; Sir John, 140
Hull, 113, 122; Charterhouse of, 37, 67; prior of, see Malleverer
Hungary, 105, 107
Hunsdon, Lord, 138n.

Inglewood Forest, 89
Ireby, Thomas, abbot of Holm Cultram, 61-2
Ishak ibn Sulaiman al Israeli, 20
Islington, 146
Ismael Sophi of Persia, 29, 82-3

James IV of Scotland, 19; James V, 43, 144
Jervaulx Abbey, 111
Jolye, Thomas, 33-4, 101-4

Kaber, 117
Katherine of Aragon, Queen, 93, 131n.
Kendal, 43
Keswick, 134n.
Kettlewell (Catelwell), 51-2, 112
Kilham, 41n.
Killerby, 73
Killinghall, 73

Kirkby, Cleveland, 43, 60
Kirkby Lonsdale, 32, 81
Kirkby Stephen, 147
Kirkland, 31, 58
Kirkoswald Castle, 146
Kite, John, Bishop of Carlisle, 40, 48, 99-100
Knowsley, 124

LANCASHIRE, 39, 123, 145
Langley, Durham, 122-3
Langwathby, 89
Latimer, see Neville; Parr, Queen Katherine
Leconfield Castle, 104
Ledes, John, *alias* Alanbridge, abbot of Byland, 57-8, 75, 78
Lee, Edward, Archbishop of York, 37-8, 67
Lee, Rowland, Bishop of Coventry and Lichfield, 39, 43, 68
Leeke, Sir John, 22; Thomas, 22
Leicester, 132n.; Leicestershire, 132
Leland, John, 49
Leo X, Pope, 39, 83, 88
Leyburn, 111
Lincoln, canons and prebends at, 40-42; Bishop of, 82
Lincolnshire, 102
Lister, Robert, 84
Londesborough (Lonnesborrow), 16, 18, 19, 29, 84, 133, 141n.
London, 19, 23, 33, 47, 49, 54, 75-6, 88, 93, 96, 99, 101, 103-4, 107, 110, 140, 145-6, 149; Bishop of, 82; Bridewell Palace, 130, 136-7, 140; Bridge, 144; Charterhouse, 24, 37; Clerkenwell, 145; Clifford's Inn, 102-3; Fleet Prison, 22; Lincoln's Inn, 73; St. Mary Graces, 75; St. Paul's, 83; Savoy, 147; White-friars, 129; see Islington; Southwark; Westminster
Longespée, Maud de, 148
Lothersdale, 26, 90
Louis II of Hungary, 105, 107
Louth, 66n.
Louvain, 40
Low Countries, 133
Lowther, family of, 49, 132; Anne, see Wibergh; Lady Dorothy, *née* Clifford, 116, 132; Sir Hugh, 21, 116, 132; Sir John, 116, 132n.; Sir John, Bart., 132
Lowther, Westmorland, 116, 132

MAGNUS, Archdeacon Thomas, 42-4, 87
Malleverer (Mauleverer), James, 67; Ralph, prior of Hull, 37, 67, 69; Sir William, 64-5, 67, 69
Maltby, 75-6
Manners, John, Roger and Thomas, 113; Thomas, Lord Ros and first Earl of Rutland, 113, 140
Marches, the Northern, 24, 46, 48, 50, 96-9, 109, 134, 141
Margaret, daughter of Henry III, 89
Margaret, Queen of Scotland, 43
Markenfield, Lady Eleanor, *née* Clifford, 131; Sir Ninian, 131n.
Markenfield Hall, 131n.
Marton, East Yorkshire, 113
Marton, Craven, 82
Marton Priory, 122
Martyn (Marton), Henry, 82
Mary I, Queen, 27, 58, 82, 132, 144, 146-7, 149
Mary, Queen of Scots, 49
Masham, 50, 112; Mashamshire, 112
Mendoza, Iñigo de, Bishop of Burgos, 105
Metcalfe, family of, 51, 118, 131, 139; Sir Christopher, 34, 50, 111-12, 118-20, 131n., 139; Edward (Edmund), 131n.; Lady Elizabeth, *née* Clifford, 52n., 111, 118, 131n., 139; Sir James, 111-12, 118-19; Robert, 55n., 131; Thomas, 118
Methley, Richard, *alias* Firth, 34-5, 71, 74
Middleham, 118-20
Middleton-in-Teesdale, 50, 64
Millom, 140n.
Mohacs, battle of, 105
Monk Bretton Priory, 37, 67, 69
Montague, Lord, 45; see Browne
Monteagle, Lord, 136n.
Moone, Richard, prior of Bolton, 85
More, Sir Thomas, 24, 130n.; William, abbot of Worcester, 39
Morlande of Winton, 117-18
Morpeth Castle, 47, 108
Mountgrace Priory, 28-30, 34-7, 62-74; see Eccleston; Methley; Norton; Wilson
Musgrave, Anne (or Agnes), *née* Wharton, 101; Lady Francis, *née* Wharton, 147; Sir Richard (16th cent.), 33-4, 101-3; Sir Richard (17th cent.), 147
Mylde (Mildy), John, 29, 68-9

NAPPA, 34, 111, 118, 120, 139n.
Neath, abbot of, 75
Netherlands, see Low Countries
Neufville, Nicholas de, 82-3
Neville, family of, 22; John, third Lord Latimer, 28, 51, 63-5, 111-12; Richard, second Lord Latimer, 28, 63, 65, 112
Newark, 42, 43
Newbiggin, Carlton in Craven, 126
Newcastle-upon-Tyne, 109, 110, 131
Nidderdale, 50
Norden Hall, 123
Norfolk, Dukes of, see Howard
Norham Castle, 19
Normanton, Thomas, *alias* Frobisher, 68
Northallerton (Alverton), 71
Northumberland, Earls of, see Percy
Norton of Bilbrough, family of, 36, 70-71; John, prior of Mountgrace, 28, 34-6, 62-3; John, see Conyers; Robert, 36, 70-71
Norton Conyers, 122
Nottingham, 54; Nottinghamshire, 54

OVERTON, 38, 78-9, 81
Oxford, Earl of, see Vere
Oxford, 41, 42; Brasenose College, 42n.; Broadgates Hall, 41; Cardinal College, 41

PACE, Richard, 39
Parkinson, Thomas, 71
Parr, family of, 99; Queen Katherine, formerly Lady Latimer, 28, 50n., 64, 99, 111; Lady Maud, 50n., 99; Sir William, 48, 99-100
Pele, Roger, abbot of Furness, 59-61
Penrith, 89
Percy, family of, 17, 19, 22, 44-8, 104, 108, 120; Henry Algernon, fifth Earl of Northumberland, 23, 41, 44-6, 104-5, 137; Henry, sixth Earl of Northumberland, 17, 23, 25, 33, 44-8, 54, 100, 105-11, 123, 125, 137-8; Katherine, *née* Spencer, Countess of Northumberland, 138; Lady Margaret, see Clifford; Mary, Countess of Northumberland, *née* Talbot, 45, 106, 110; Sir Thomas, 45
Perkynson, William, 95
Philip II of Spain, 144, 146
Pickering, 41n.
Pigot, Sir Ranulph, 70
Pocklington, 41n., 85
Popeley, Henry, 21
Port, Sir John, 36, 70-71
Proctor, John, 60
Prudhoe (Prydow) Castle, 110-11
Pudsey, family of, 21, 113, 132n.; Elizabeth, *née* Scrope, 113; Florence, see Clifford; Henry, 132n.; Thomas, 113
Pulleyn, John, 73

QUEEN'S HAIMS, 89

RAYDALE (Radale), 119
Rhodes, a Knight of, 64, 66
Richard III, earlier Duke of Gloucester, 18, 135
Richmond, Henry Fitzroy, Duke of, 41, 43, 48, 99, 116
Richmond and Derby, Margaret, Countess of, 129
Richmond, 112, 118; Liberty of, 118; Richmondshire, 34, 49, 51, 112, 119, 121
Rievaulx Abbey, 36n.
Ripley, George, 20
Ripon, 131n.
Robinson, Elizabeth, 38, 78
Roche Abbey, 32, 37-8, 75-7; abbot of, see Cundall
Rome, 39, 105, 107; Castello St. Angelo, 106-7; St. Peter's, 105; Vatican, 105
Roper, William, 130n.
Ros, Thomas, fifth Lord, 113; see Manners
Rose Castle, 40
Rowcliffe, Anne, see Clifford; Sir Henry, 139
Rutland, Edmund, Earl of, 128, 133; Thomas, first Earl of, see Manners

ST. JOHN, of Bletsoe, family of, 144; Anne, see Clifford; Sir John, the elder, 129; the younger, 129
St. Paul (Sampoll, etc.), family of, 102; John, 102-3
Salkeld, Henry, 30, 97; Lancelot, prior of Carlisle, 31, 58-9
Salkeld, 89
Sandes, Lord, 106
Savage, Thomas, Archbishop of York, 29-30, 42, 44, 90-92
Scarborough, 101, 139n.; Castle, 122
Scotby, 89

Scotland, 43, 83, 89, 97-8, 109, 131n., 141
Scott, Sir Walter, 33
Scrope of Bolton, family of, 17, 49, 51, 122; Elizabeth, see Pudsey; Henry, seventh Lord, 33, 49, 114-17, 121; Henry, ninth Lord, 27, 51n.; John, eighth Lord, 33-4, 49-52, 114, 117-23, 139; John, son of the eighth Lord, 122; Lady Katherine, *née* Clifford, later Cholmeley, 33, 49-53, 111-14, 139; Lady Mabel, *née* Dacre, 116
Scrope of Masham, family of, 112; Thomas, fifth Lord, 73
Seamer, 67
Semer Water, 49
Sessay, 43, 44
Settle, 131n.
Shap Abbey, 21, 31, 77-8, 91, 129, 136; abbot of, see Bagot
Sheen, Charterhouse of, 37
Sherrington, Sir William, 102-3
Shrewsbury, Earl of, see Talbot
Sibthorpe College, 43
Siggiswick, family of, 51; Mr., 111; Richard, 111-12
Sinningthwaite Priory, 67
Skelton in Cleveland, 53
Skipton-in-Craven, 18, 26, 30, 51, 59, 60, 112, 115; Castle, 16, 18-20, 24, 29, 51-2, 60, 90-92, 135, 137, 141-2, 146-7; church, 24, 130, 137-8, 142-8, 150; honor of, 128, 133, 136, 142-3; school, 101; vicars of, 17, 24, 33-4, 101-4
Sleningford, 113
Snape, 51, 111-12
Snarford, 102
Sneaton, 113
Snotterton, 64
Solway Moss, 33, 50, 101
Somerset, Duke of, see Beaufort; Protector (Hertford), 34, 50, 102-4
Somerset Herald, 25n.
Southwark, 141, 144; St. Mary Overies, 141, 144; Suffolk Palace, 141, 144
Southwell, Robert, 45, 60
Sowerby, Cumberland, 31, 77, 89
Spencer, Earl, 16; Katherine, see Percy; Eleanor, *née* Beaufort, 138; Margaret, 138n.; Sir Robert, 138
Spencercombe, 138n.
Spenser, Mr., 114
Spinelli, Thomas, 105
Stanley, family of, 17; Edward, third Earl of Derby, 30, 60, 123-4, 145; Ferdinando, fifth Earl of Derby, 145; Henry, Lord Strange, later fourth Earl of Derby, 27, 138, 144-5, 149; James, seventh Earl of Derby, 145; Margaret, Countess of Derby, *née* Clifford, 138, 142, 144-5, 149; Sir William, 18, 135; William, sixth Earl of Derby, 145
Stapleton, Sir Brian, 67; Isabel, 67; Joan, 67; William, the elder, 37, 67, 69; the younger, 67
Steeple Claydon, 149n.
Steeton, 113
Stewart, Sir James, Master of Blantyre, 146n.
Stokesley, 41n.
Strangeways (Strangwiche), Sir James, 73, 113; Sir Thomas, 73
Streatlam, 131n.
Suffolk, Duke of, see Brandon
Surrey, Earl of, see Howard

Talbot, family of, 113; Lady Elizabeth, see Dacre; George, fourth Earl of Shrewsbury, 23-4, 45, 106, 110, 145; Lady Margaret, see Clifford; Lady Mary, see Percy; Thomas, 21, 132n.
Tankard, William, 102-3
Teesdale, 63-4, 71-2
Tempest, Roger, 60-61; Sir Thomas, 119
Tenbury (Temedbury), 26, 148-9
Thirkeld, see Threlkeld
Thirsk, 50
Thomson, Stephen, 54, 125-6
Thoresby (Thursby), family of, 122; Ralph, 20; William, 50, 122
Thoresby, 50
Thornton, William, abbot of St. Mary's, York, 38-9, 78-81
Thornton, near Pocklington, 85-6
Thorpe Perrow, 51, 112
Threlkeld (Thirkeld), Anne, 132; Sir Lancelot, 18, 19, 67, 132, 134; Lady Margaret, see Clifford
Threlkeld (Thrilcot), 134
Thrimby, 97
Topcliffe (Topliffe), Mr., 69
Topcliffe (Topliffe), 110
Tournai, 82
Towton, battle of, 18, 133
Tubley, Stephen, 54, 126

Tudor, Mary, Queen of France, Duchess of Suffolk, 24, 138, 141, 143-4
Tunstall, Cuthbert, Bishop of Durham, 100-101, 105
Tunstall (Durham), 64
Turk, the, 29, 82-3, 107
Tuxford, 32, 75-6

ULLESKELFE, prebend of, 41
Utley, 26, 90

VATICAN, see Rome.
Vavasour, family of, 33
Vere, John de, fifteenth Earl of Oxford, 106
Vescy (Vesey), Sir Henry Bromflete, first Lord, 19, 85, 129, 133-4; Margaret, see Clifford
Veteripont (Vipont), peerage of, 132n.; family of, 18, 127; Isabella de, see Clifford.
Vipont, see Veteripont

WALBURN, 111
Waller, Edward, 117-18; Robert, 117; Thomas, 117
Wanless, 118
Warcop, 31, 57
Warham, William, Archbishop of Canterbury, 83, 105, 110
Warter Priory, 80
Waverley, abbot of, 75
Wensleydale, 49, 51, 111, 118, 139n.
Westminster, 90; Abbey, 145; Whitehall, 144; York Place, 47, 90n., 106
West Newton Grange, 139n.
Westmorland, 16, 18, 19, 21, 24, 27n., 31, 33, 49, 57, 77, 84, 97, 102-3, 116, 128, 134-6, 139, 143-4, 146-7, 149
Wetherby, 139n.
Whalley, Edmund, abbot of St. Mary's, York, 79-80
Wharfe, River, 19
Wharton, Lady Frances, *née* Clifford, 146; Frances, see Musgrave; Sir George, 146; Margaret, see Wotton; Philip, Lord Wharton, the elder, 146; the younger, 146; Thomas, 30, 97; Sir Thomas, later first Lord Wharton, 25, 30, 33-4, 45, 48, 101, 108; Sir Thomas (17th cent.), 146
Wharton Hall, 146
Wheatly Hill, 64
Whinfell Forest (Wynfild), 29, 88, 104
Whitaker, T. D., 16, 20, 26
Whitby, 52, 113
Whorlton Castle, 73
Wibergh (Wybere), family of, 49, 116; Anne, *née* Lowther, 49, 116-17; Thomas, 49, 116-17
Wighill, 37
Wilson, John, prior of Mountgrace, 28-30, 34, 36-7, 62-73
Winchester, Bishop of, see Fox
Windsor, 42, 80, 93
Winterburn, 30, 60-61, 123-4
Winton, Kirkby Stephen, 117-18
Woburn, abbot of, 75
Wolsey, Cardinal, 17, 22-4, 29, 32, 39-42, 44-8, 82-3, 88-90, 94, 99, 105-7
Woodhall, Wensleydale, 118
Woodsome, 64
Worcestershire, 26, 148
Wordsworth, William, 18, 19
Wotton, Edward, Lord, 146; Lady Margaret, *née* Wharton, 146
Wressle Castle, 104-5

YANWATH, 18, 134n.
York, 41, 42, 43, 50, 85, 87, 100-101, 119-21, 126, 148; Archbishops of, see Savage, Bainbridge, Wolsey, Lee, Holgate, Grindal; archdeacon of, dean of, see Higdon; Corpus Christi Guild, 67; diocese of, 42-3, 84-6; Minster, 42n., 43-4, 101; prebends in, 39, 40, 41, 93; recorders of, 68, 73, 102; treasurer of, 42; St. Leonard's Hospital, 42; St. Mary's Abbey, 31, 32, 38-9, 44, 78-81; abbots of, see Thornton, Whalley; St. Saviour's, 37, 68; St. Sepulchre's College, 43; town clerk of, 73
York Place, see Westminster
Yorkshire, 19, 22, 25, 27-8, 35, 41, 43, 48, 60, 70, 129-30, 139; East Riding of, 18, 32, 42, 104, 113, 122; M.P.s for, 101-2; High Sheriffs of, 22, 73